Historical Association Studies

The Cold War
1945–1965

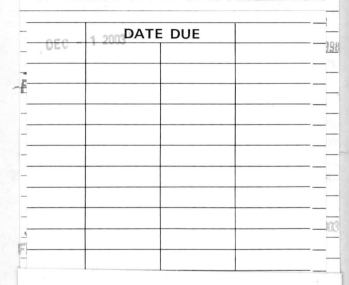

The Cold War
1945–1965

Joseph Smith

Basil Blackwell

Copyright © Joseph Smith 1989

First published 1989

Basil Blackwell Ltd
108 Cowley Road, Oxford, OX4 1JF, UK

Basil Blackwell Inc.
432 Park Avenue South, Suite 1503
New York, NY 10016, USA

British Library Cataloguing in Publication Data
Smith, Joseph
   The Cold War: 1945–1965—(Historical
   Association Studies)
   1. Soviet Union. Foreign relations with
   United States, 1945–1970. 2. United States.
   Foreign relations with the Soviet Union,
   1945–1970
   I. Title II. Series
   327.47073
   ISBN 0–631–15816–2

Library of Congress Cataloging in Publication Data
Smith, Joseph, 1945–
   The Cold War, 1945–1965/Joseph Smith.
     p. cm.—(Historical Association studies)
   Bibliography: p.
   ISBN 0–631–15816–2
   1. World politics—1945–1955. 2. World politics—1955–1965.
I. Title II. Series.
D842.5.S57 1989   88–34628
909.82—dc 19   CIP

Typeset in 10 on 11½pt Erhardt by Footnote Graphics, Warminster, Wilts
Printed in Great Britain by Whitstable Litho Ltd., Whitstable, Kent

Contents

Preface

The close of the Second World War in 1945 is a convenient starting point for this short study of the Cold War. The date at which to end is not so straightforward. I chose 1965 because it represents a point in the mid-1960s when the bipolar world gave way to a more diverse international order. For reasons of continuity, however, chapter 3 takes the story of American involvement in Vietnam up to 1975.

The role of the United States looms large throughout this study. This reflects the predominant economic and military power wielded by that nation during the period from 1945 to 1965. The American perspective is further reinforced by the fact that research and writing on the Cold War is indebted to the opening of American archives and the ensuing historical debate which has been at its most lively and incisive in the West. Unfortunately, a similar debate has not taken place in the Soviet Union and that country's policy remains obscured by lack of access to the Soviet archives.

Joseph Smith
University of Exeter

1 Beginning of the Cold War

Rise of the Superpowers

Despite their enormous size and resources, the United States and the Soviet Union assumed a peripheral role in international affairs between the two world wars. American diplomacy traditionally emphasized separation from the Old World and pursued a policy known as 'isolationism'. Although a large part of the Soviet Union actually adjoined Europe in geographical terms, the Bolshevist state headed by Stalin also preferred little direct contact with European capitalist governments. Consequently, both the United States and the Soviet Union were diplomatic bystanders in the wrangles which increasingly wracked Europe during the 1930s. The great European powers of Britain, France, Germany, and Italy were accustomed to dominating world affairs and their telegraph wires hummed as they squabbled over the Sudetenland and the Polish corridor. However, when war ultimately erupted in September 1939, it soon expanded beyond the continent of Europe and acquired global dimensions.

Just over two decades earlier the United States had become involved in the First World War. Led by President Woodrow Wilson, the American people had sought 'to make the world safe for democracy'. But the peace settlement brought only disillusionment. The traditional American aversion to entangling alliances was soon restored as the United States withdrew into isolationism and sought to stay neutral in European disputes. 'Never Again' was a popular slogan of the 1930s and was reaffirmed by the cries of 'America First' in 1940.

Neutrality was, however, challenged by increasing anxiety that

Europe might fall under the control of totalitarian dictators. In January 1941 President Franklin D. Roosevelt sought to alert American opinion to the attendant dangers when he stressed the urgent need to defend the 'Four Freedoms': freedom of speech and of worship, freedom from want and from fear. In a statement of what would become the policy of 'Lend–Lease', Roosevelt told the democratic nations of the world: 'We Americans are vitally concerned in your defense of freedom. We are putting forth our energies, our resources and our organizing powers to give you the strength to regain and maintain a free world. We shall send you, in ever-increasing numbers, ships, planes, tanks, guns' (Siracusa, 1978, p. 5). But despite Roosevelt's unequivocal pledge of support, the United States still hesitated to enter the war formally. However, the attack by Japan on Pearl Harbor in December 1941 and Germany's declaration of war on the United States only a few days later brought an abrupt end to the period of American neutrality.

Whereas Roosevelt had consistently denounced the Nazi regime, Stalin adopted a more ambiguous attitude and initially viewed the crisis over Poland as an opportunity to expand Soviet borders to the west. The Non-Aggression Pact was signed with Germany in August 1939 and allowed the Soviet Union to seize the Baltic states and part of eastern Poland. Moreover, as the world's only socialist state dedicated to the ultimate triumph of communism, Stalin was not unhappy to see the capitalist powers fight amongst themselves. But he appeared guilty of miscalculation and military unpreparedness when Hitler launched his massive invasion of the Soviet Union in June 1941. A struggle for national survival ensued in which Stalin was soon pleading with the West for assistance.

Despite granting diplomatic recognition to the Soviet Union in 1933, Americans were traditionally hostile to communism. It was viewed as an alien ideology which suppressed political, economic, and religious freedom. But the threat of Nazism was even more alarming. In the immediate aftermath of the attack on Pearl Harbor, Americans demanded revenge against Japan. However, Roosevelt and his advisers regarded Hitler as the greater danger and consequently insisted on pursuing a Europe-first military strategy. Stalin was led to believe that a 'second front' would be speedily opened in Western Europe, but this was not judged to be militarily feasible. So long as the Western allies were unable to strike directly at Nazi power, the eastern front assumed crucial strategic significance. By recommending that Lend–Lease be extended to the Soviet Union, Roosevelt showed his agreement with Churchill that Stalin was 'a welcome guest at [a] hungry table' (Dallek, 1979, p. 293). Soon it would be argued not only that the United States and the Soviet Union were fighting on the same side, but also that they shared the same goals. The common fear of Hitler thereby brought together an improbable alliance comprising the forces of British imperialism, American capitalism, and Soviet communism.

The ensuing global struggle was one of total war in which the superior resources of the 'Big Three' assured them ultimate military victory. In fact, a new historical epoch was under way. After the self-destruction wreaked by the 'Thirty Years War' from 1914 to 1945, the fortunes of a weak and divided Europe were to be dictated by powers outside the mainstream of European history. In 1945 Germany and Italy were defeated nations. Their economies were devastated and their people cowed by military occupation and foreign administration. France was liberated, but was only belatedly admitted to the circle of the great powers. This recognition was grudgingly given by the Big Three and could scarcely hide the scars of French military defeat, economic decline, and the humiliation brought about by the Vichy regime.

After standing alone against the might of Nazi Germany in 1940–1, Britain emerged from the war with considerable pride and sense of achievement. British courage was personified by Churchill whose international reputation was at its zenith. The British prime minister deservedly took the centre of the world stage along with Roosevelt and Stalin. Signs of Britain's decline were, however, apparent throughout the war and were merely disguised by what seemed to be her finest hour. Churchill had desperately sought American assistance in 1940 because he believed it was the only way to ensure the survival of the British empire. American intervention did secure ultimate military victory over the Axis powers, but at the price of Britain's economic and military subordination to the United States. The enormous cost of war compelled Britain to incur vast new debts and liquidate so much of her assets that a superpower role was beyond British resources. Postwar events such as the urgent need for an American loan and the granting of independence to India in 1947 symbolized the passing of an era.

3

However, the transition was not always clearly perceived by contemporaries and was masked by Britain's colonial empire and her claim to a 'special relationship' with the United States. Consequently, for some time Britain's actual power was considerably overestimated by America, by Russia, and by Britain herself.

The Soviet Union suffered the heaviest losses of any country during the war and was economically crippled in 1945. More than 20 million people had died, while agriculture and industry lay devastated. Only by supreme military and economic sacrifice had the Soviet people rolled back the Nazi war machine to the German capital itself. Not only was Mother Russia saved, but the dramatic eclipse of Nazi Germany also created a vacuum of power in Eastern Europe. The Soviet Union found herself in a position of unaccustomed and almost complete dominance. Under the leadership of Stalin, the Soviet Union soon demonstrated that she possessed the necessary political will and organization to direct her military power, human resources, and economic potential to claim equal superpower status with the United States.

The advance of the Soviet Union was overshadowed by the even more remarkable rise of the United States from isolation to world leadership. In marked contrast to the other belligerents, American wartime losses and sacrifices were disproportionately small. Indeed, the United States might actually be said to have benefited from the war. Not only had population increased from 131 to 140 million, but the gross national product had soared from $90 billion in 1939 to $211 billion in 1945 (Paterson, 1979, p. 15). The United States had replaced Britain as indisputably the world's leading economic power and supplier of credit. Moreover, she possessed a vast military establishment, which in 1945 also acquired the monopoly of atomic weapons. Although he feared a postwar desire for a return to isolationism, Roosevelt firmly believed that America both needed and was obliged to restore the world to peace and prosperity. It was a vision which he frequently proclaimed in his public speeches and statements.

The immediate task, however, was to win the war. Roosevelt considered military cooperation between the Big Three so crucial that he avoided or tactfully ignored potential disagreements. A friendly atmosphere pervaded the summit meetings held at Tehran in 1943 and at Yalta in February 1945. The president was

4

particularly keen to establish a special personal relationship with the Soviet leader. On his return from Tehran, he told the American people: 'I got along fine with Marshal Stalin ... and I believe that we are going to get along very well with him and the Russian people – very well indeed' (Dallek, 1979, p. 439). The image later promoted of Stalin as 'Uncle Joe' was intended to be reassuring and implied that the prospects for future cooperation were bright.

Roosevelt did not reveal publicly, however, that he had given Stalin what amounted to a virtual acknowledgement that Eastern Europe was a Soviet sphere of influence. The advance of the Red Army into Poland brought this matter to the fore in 1944. Churchill made the restoration of Polish freedom a major issue and reminded his wartime partners that Britain and France had gone to war over this very issue in 1939. But Poland was also the gateway to Moscow for foreign invaders. Stalin was in no mood to compromise over what he described as 'not only a question of honour for Russia, but one of life and death' (Dallek, 1979, p. 513). The Soviet leader insisted on retaining the areas of east Prussia which he had gained from the Non-Aggression Pact with Hitler in 1939. This entailed giving Poland territorial compensation by pushing her western border to the Neisse line. Moreover, Stalin would not permit the return to power of those Polish exiles who had formed a government in London.

Despite British grumbles, the Americans remained quiescent and allowed the extension of communist control over Poland. Roosevelt wished to avoid Poland becoming a divisive issue between the allies. Moreover, there was little else that could be done so long as Poland was occupied by the Red Army and allied troops were hundreds of miles away. The issue appeared to be resolved at the Yalta conference by the 'Declaration on Liberated Europe', which sought to provide for 'free and unfettered elections' (Thomas, 1986, pp. 186–7). But this merely proved to be a diplomatic compromise that allowed both sides to interpret 'democracy' in the way which best suited them. The Soviet authorities made token gestures of permitting members of the exiled Polish government to take up political activities, but communists remained in effective control.

The euphoria of victory over Germany in 1945 moderated dissensions. At Yalta the Big Three leaders casually talked of

5

allocating to each other their respective spheres of influence. Roosevelt was unwilling to give any American postwar commitments to Europe and implied that America would speedily disengage from Europe. In his opinion, America was not a European power and her troops would be out of Europe within two years. The implication was that Churchill and Stalin would be left to decide the exact nature of Europe's fate.

American policy, however, was ambivalent. Roosevelt's private acknowledgement of spheres of influence was contradicted by his public speeches, which stressed Wilsonian ideas of 'open' diplomacy and self-determination for all nations. While America might choose to run down her military power after the war, she did not intend to surrender her new-found world influence. Roosevelt and his successor, Harry Truman, posited a concept of a liberal world order headed by the United Nations, International Monetary Fund, and World Bank, which would promote and guarantee world security and recovery. Under American tutelage, the Big Three would work together in this common endeavour.

At the Potsdam conference in July 1945 there was a change in the composition of the Big Three. Truman had succeeded Roosevelt and Attlee replaced Churchill during the meeting. Nevertheless, the rhetoric of wartime alliance was reaffirmed. The war was won, but a common desire existed to ensure peace and to avoid a third world war. The former great powers of Europe anxiously awaited the decisions to be made at councils from which they were absent. In principle, the superpowers were in agreement, but difficulties soon surfaced over the future of Germany.

The Problem of Germany

In the spring of 1945 the Third Reich was effectively abolished when the advancing armies of the Big Three triumphantly joined together on the plains of Germany. The victors found themselves presiding over a nation in ruins and a people in despair. Despite the local chaos and desolation, the transition from war to peace proceeded more smoothly than expected. Germany was placed under military rule and divided into zones broadly reflecting the positions drawn up at the close of hostilities by the occupying

6

armies. The Russians were stationed in the east, the Americans took the south while the British established themselves in the northwest. The main agricultural region was therefore controlled by the Soviets, while the industrial heartland of the Ruhr was allocated to Britain. A later quip was that the Americans were left with the scenery. On the insistence of Britain and the United States, France was given parts of the British and American zones. The city of Berlin was similarly divided into four separate sectors and became the headquarters of the Allied Control Council which was established to rule Germany.

The goal and priority of the Big Three during the war had been to defeat Germany. There was, however, no such clear purpose regarding the postwar future of that country. The problem was simply too complex and too important to permit of a quick solution. Moreover, in contrast to Poland or Japan, no one power possessed a preponderating military influence. The imposition of separate zones of occupation was merely a practical necessity and was seen as a temporary arrangement pending a full-scale conference to effect a definitive peace treaty. The onus was upon the Big Three, especially the two superpowers, to work together to achieve a settlement that would have a crucial effect upon the future relations of Europe and world peace.

In 1945 a general belief prevailed among the victors that the German people had been treated too leniently at the end of the First World War and that this mistake should not be repeated. 'The fact that they are a defeated nation, collectively and individually,' President Roosevelt declared, 'must be so impressed upon them that they will hesitate to start any new war' (Dallek, 1979, p. 472). The instinct to take revenge and mete out punishment was evident in the denazification programmes which were instituted within each zone. High-ranking Nazis faced the severest penalties, while millions of lesser officials were treated as criminals and shown little sympathy.

Linked to the question of punishment was the common desire of the Big Three to prevent the resurgence of Germany as a military threat. They were unanimous that the German armed forces should be permanently disbanded. Some consideration was also briefly given at the wartime conferences to dismembering Germany into several smaller and separate states. Although the Big Three

7

recognized that Germany must lose territory in the east to the Soviet Union and Poland, they demonstrated no desire for further territorial aggrandizement at Germany's expense. The temporary nature of the zonal division was reaffirmed and it was anticipated that Germany would soon be reunified as a single nation-state.

The debate over economic policy was more controversial and ultimately proved divisive. Although they agreed that Germany should be kept economically weak, the powers were uncertain how this was to be achieved. The American secretary of the treasury, Henry Morgenthau, argued in 1944 that Germany be deindustrialized and reduced to what amounted to a medieval pastoral economy. Although the 'Morgenthau Plan' never became official American policy, its influence was reflected in the decision to regard the German people as a captured enemy nation who should expect to be maintained at a low standard of living for the immediate future.

The outlines of a common economic strategy emerged as the Big Three agreed to dismantle Germany's warmaking industries and to permit economic production at low levels so as to allow only a minimal standard of living for the local population. But implementation of this policy soon became entangled with Stalin's insistence that Germany pay large reparations in the shape of the removal of industrial equipment and transfer of raw materials to assist Soviet domestic reconstruction. At the Yalta conference Foreign Minister Molotov proposed that Germany pay $20 billion of which the Soviet Union would receive half.

Not having suffered bombing and invasion, the Americans were lukewarm to the idea of reparations, which they believed had not only proved costly and troublesome during the 1920s, but had also contributed directly to the rise of Hitler. Moreover, if the United States wished an economically prosperous Germany to reappear, a policy of rehabilitation rather than repression was preferable. Officials at the State Department urged the former, while the Treasury and the War Department favoured the latter. President Roosevelt appeared uncertain and provided no clear direction. He preferred to concentrate on winning the war. Until that was achieved, political decisions were postponed.

Nevertheless, while the United States wanted no reparations for herself, they could hardly be denied to the Soviets after their

8

immense wartime sacrifices. Roosevelt admitted as much at the Yalta conference, although his untimely death in April 1945 meant that the actual task of working out a reparations agreement fell to his successor, Harry Truman. Although the new president was inexperienced in foreign affairs and did not attempt to disguise his hostility towards communism, he was willing to agree to reparations in principle.

Indeed, American officials believed that they possessed considerable bargaining power over the Soviets since the latter were desperate for the industrial goods and equipment which were largely located in the Ruhr. At the Potsdam conference Secretary of State James Byrnes sought to moderate Soviet demands by avoiding naming an exact total figure. Instead, he worked out a compromise by which the Soviets would draw the bulk of reparations from their own zone while being given only limited amounts of industrial material from the West. The outcome signified the American desire to restrict, if not exclude, Soviet contact with the Western zones. In effect, Germany was being partitioned by the superpowers. This was implicit in the question posed by Foreign Minister Molotov: 'Would not the Secretary's suggestion mean that each country would have a free hand in their own zones and would act entirely independently of the others?' Byrnes acknowledged that 'the Soviet Union would take what it wished from its own zone' (Kuklick, 1972, p. 155).

In contrast to the harsh reparations policy exacted by the Soviets, the American military authorities adopted a humane and sympathetic attitude towards the defeated enemy. 'God, I hate the Germans,' General Eisenhower had once written, but the sight of GIs distributing candy bars and chewing gum to German children made him relax the regulations prohibiting the fraternization of American troops with the local population (Ambrose, 1983b, pp. 422–3). Although the Potsdam formula required that the German living standard be kept low, American officials became alarmed by the growing evidence of shortages of food and fuel. The dilemma was compounded by the onset of winter and the daily arrival of thousands of refugees fleeing from the East. The lack of agricultural capacity in their zone compelled the American authorities to resort to importing food and raw materials from the United States. Not only was this expensive, but unless steps were taken to revive the German economy it threatened to become an intolerable burden for the American taxpayer.

9

The American deputy military governor, General Lucius Clay, considered that the food crisis could only become worse unless a centralized administrative agency was established to ensure the efficient interzonal allocation and distribution of economic resources. In his view the major stumbling block was not so much the Soviets as France. The latter sought to keep Germany permanently weak not only by demanding heavy reparations, but also by resisting all attempts to make the Allied Control Council an effective instrument of central government. In May 1946 General Clay sought to force discussion of the whole issue by halting the transfer of reparations from the American zone. While France still remained intransigent, the Soviets were stung into protesting that Clay's action was 'unlawful' (Gaddis, 1972, p. 330).

A constructive response was, however, forthcoming from Britain whose government shared American suspicions that the Soviets were using the reparations issue to keep Germany economically weak and consequently vulnerable to communist subversion and ultimate control. Moreover, faced with the same dilemma as the United States in having to feed the Germans in her zone, Britain regarded economic cooperation as the quickest means to mitigate an escalating financial burden. Britain desperately needed American dollars to finance imports, while the United States required coal and raw materials from the British zone. Anglo-American cooperation was formalized in mid-1946 by the decision to combine their two zones into a separate economic unit. The new entity was called 'Bizonia' and came into being in January 1947.

At the Yalta conference in February 1945 President Roosevelt had predicted that American troops would be withdrawn from Europe within two years of the end of the war. Eighteen months later Secretary of State Byrnes made an important speech at Stuttgart in which he indicated that the Potsdam agreements concerning Germany had broken down. The United States had withdrawn into isolation in 1919, but Byrnes warned: 'We will not again make that mistake. We intend to continue our interest in the affairs of Europe and of the world' (Schlesinger, 1983, I, p. 436). The implication that Germany was to be rehabilitated and not repressed was underlined by Byrnes's successor, General Marshall, who noted in March 1947 that his government was 'opposed to policies which will continue Germany as a congested slum or an economic

10

poorhouse in the center of Europe' (1983, I, p. 459). In effect, the United States was prepared to lead and finance the reconstruction of Germany so as to provide a buffer against Soviet expansionism.

Clay's virtual ultimatum in May 1946 effectively brought an end to the frustrating saga of reparations. The Soviets felt aggrieved since no more than $25–50 million in goods was transferred from the Western zones to the Soviet Union (Kuklick, 1972, pp. 233–4). Moreover, the Western powers accused the Soviets of systematic looting of the Eastern zone. The meetings of foreign ministers at Moscow in March 1947 and later at London in November only resulted in a diplomatic impasse. The great peace conference to decide the future of Germany was abandoned. Instead, the temporary military boundaries drawn up in 1945 became permanent borders in 1949 when the French zone joined with Bizonia. The division of Germany into two separate and hostile blocs underlined the state of acute rivalry between the two superpowers and demonstrated that the wartime partnership could not persist into peacetime.

The Containment of Communism

The conflict between the superpowers over Germany was mirrored elsewhere. The ruthless establishment of a communist government in Poland aroused American charges that Stalin had gone back on his undertaking given at Yalta to allow 'free elections'. The issue was bluntly raised by Truman at his notorious meeting with Molotov in April 1945. 'I have never been talked to like that in my life,' complained the Soviet foreign minister. Truman brusquely retorted: 'Carry out your agreements and you won't get talked to like that' (Truman, 1955, p. 85). An official reply was soon forthcoming from Stalin which tersely declared that 'the Soviet Government cannot agree to the existence in Poland of a Government hostile to it' (Siracusa, 1978, p. 88). Soviet security considerations were hardly to be swayed by rhetoric no matter how tough.

The United States was able, however, to exert more tangible influence in the crisis which emerged over Iran. The country had been under joint Anglo-Soviet occupation since 1941 and both nations had agreed to withdraw by 2 March 1946. But reports of Soviet troop movements in the northern province of Azerbaijan suggested that Stalin intended to violate the wartime understanding. A remote part of the world suddenly acquired international significance. 'Our continued access to oil in the Middle East is especially threatened by Soviet penetration into Iran,' noted one alarmed White House official (Krock, 1968, p. 471). The Truman administration became determined to resist what was perceived as deliberate Soviet aggression. American diplomatic support was given to the Shah's decision to send troops to the northern border and also to raise the issue at the United Nations. Secretary of State Byrnes seized the opportunity to go before the Security Council and publicly condemn Soviet imperialism. Although the Soviet representative, Andrei Gromyko, chose to stage a dramatic walk out from the chamber, the Soviets quickly defused the crisis by agreeing to pull their military forces out of Iran.

The vigorous American response towards events in Iran reflected the growing conviction in Washington that the Soviet Union had become an enemy of the United States and that her insatiable appetite for expansion must be checked. Especially influential were the ideas of George Kennan, the former chargé d'affaires at the American embassy in Moscow. In February 1946 he despatched to the State Department what became known as the 'Long Telegram'. In it he warned of the danger of 'acting chummy' with the Soviets and explained that they were 'committed fanatically to the belief that with [the] US there can be no permanent modus vivendi' (Kennan, 1968, pp. 291, 557). The analysis merely confirmed and reinforced the already strong anti-Soviet prejudices of many Washington officials. A special report prepared for President Truman by his White House aide, Clark Clifford, stated that 'compromise and concessions are considered by the Soviets, to be evidence of weakness'. The United States must avoid the error of 'appeasement' and should even be prepared to go to war if necessary to resist Stalin's ambitions for world conquest (Krock, 1968, pp. 477–8).

In an article published in July 1947 Kennan stressed the need for 'a long-term, patient but firm and vigilant containment of Russian expansive tendencies' (Kennan, 1968, p. 359). The term 'containment' was soon widely adopted to describe the aim of American policy in its dealings with the Soviet Union. In fact, the attention of the American public had already been drawn to the new strategy by events in Iran and especially the eastern Mediterranean. This latter area was traditionally within the British sphere of influence, but Britain informed the State Department on 21 February 1947 that she could no longer afford to sustain a military role in Greece and Turkey beyond 31 March. The spectre of Soviet aggression loomed large in the minds of Washington officials who feared that communists were responsible for the civil war that was raging in Greece. Moreover, American suspicions of a conspiracy masterminded from Moscow appeared to be confirmed by simultaneous Soviet pressure on Turkey for naval access to the Mediterranean.

A sense of urgency and excitement permeated the Truman administration. Prompt and decisive action was considered crucial. But doubts were expressed whether the American public and Congress would support the United States replacing Britain in a distant area of the world where Americans historically had little interest or direct involvement. Consequently, the communist bogey was overstated to alert congressional and public opinion to the danger. The lines of battle were eloquently drawn by Truman in his address to Congress on 12 March:

At the present moment in world history nearly every nation must choose between alternative ways of life. The choice is too often not a free one. One way of life is based upon the will of the majority, and is distinguished by free institutions, representative government, free elections, guaranties of individual liberty, freedom of speech and religion and freedom from political oppression. The second way of life is based upon the will of a minority forcibly imposed on the majority. It relies upon terror and oppression, a controlled press and radio, framed elections and the suppression of personal freedoms. I believe that it must be the policy of the United States to support free peoples who are resisting attempted subjugation by armed minorities or by outside pressures. (Schlesinger, 1983, I, p. 113)

Congress speedily assented to Truman's request for the relatively small amount of $400 million to save Greece and Turkey from communism. But the pledge to support 'free peoples' had much wider ramifications. The president's speech was referred to as the

13

'Truman Doctrine', and its impact and significance soon extended far beyond the eastern Mediterranean. The same affliction of poverty, which bred despair and undermined democratic institutions in Greece, was also evident throughout Europe. In April 1947 Secretary of State Marshall returned from Europe with the gloomy diagnosis that 'the patient is sinking while the doctors deliberate' (Halle, 1967, p. 167). State Department officials carefully observed the political activities of communist parties, especially those in France and Italy. They feared that total economic collapse was imminent and would be followed by political revolution. A massive programme of financial aid was urgently required to stimulate economic revival and thereby relieve the sense of hopelessness and anxiety over communist encroachment. In a speech at Harvard on 5 June Marshall announced his government's intention to promote the economic recovery of Europe. 'It is logical', he declared, 'that the United States should do whatever it is able to do to assist in the return of normal economic health in the world, without which there can be no political stability and no assured peace' (Schlesinger, 1983, I, p. 53).

The funds for the recovery programme were estimated at several billions of dollars and would require the approval of an American Congress which was not only economy-minded, but also contained a Republican majority. Passage was therefore by no means guaranteed. A public relations campaign ensued in which administration spokesmen emphasized the seriousness of Europe's economic plight and how this acutely jeopardized the stability of democratic governments. Calculated appeals were also made to American economic self-interest by pointing out how increased trade would directly benefit American exports. Congressmen were reassured by statements that American financial assistance would be contingent upon European cooperation and self-help.

Led by the governments of Britain and France, the countries of Western Europe enthusiastically welcomed what the British foreign minister, Ernest Bevin, later described as 'a lifeline to sinking men' (*New York Times*, 2 April 1949). Faced with acute shortages of food and fuel, rising inflation, and a projected annual deficit in balance of payments of more than $5 billion, Europe was desperate for American dollars. French concern surfaced, however, over the American insistence that Germany be included in the recovery plan.

14

'Without a revival of German production', affirmed Kennan, 'there can be no revival of Europe's economy' (LaFeber, 1976, p. 63). The need for immediate aid and the tacit promise that substantial sums would be specially earmarked for France persuaded the latter to acquiesce in Germany's inclusion.

Even more controversial was the prospect of Soviet participation. Although the recovery programme was intended to contain communist expansion, Marshall had initially stressed that it was open to all European countries, including those under communist governments: 'Our policy is directed not against any country or doctrine but against hunger, poverty, desperation and chaos' (Schlesinger, 1983, I, p. 53). Indeed, the Soviets took Marshall at his word and accepted the invitation made by the foreign ministers of Britain and France to attend a Three-power preliminary conference to discuss the American proposals. In June 1947 Molotov arrived at Paris accompanied by no less than 89 advisers. It seemed that the Soviets regarded the Marshall Plan as an alternative to German reparations. But the aid was not without strings since inclusion in the recovery programme would require the disclosure of economic information to the United States. The prospect of American supervision and interference in the Soviet economy was unacceptable to Molotov. After only a few days he abruptly withdrew from the conference, accusing the United States of a plot to infringe the sovereignty of independent nations. In his opinion, the proposed scheme was a cunning attempt to rescue American capitalism by economically enslaving Europe.

The Soviets also saw the Marshall Plan as a serious threat to their control of Eastern Europe. Poland, Czechoslovakia, and Hungary had already expressed their intention to attend the full-scale conference to be held at Paris in late July. Pressure was now applied from Moscow to persuade those governments to join the Soviet Union in boycotting the meeting. The Soviets proceeded to stage their own rival conference in September at which the Communist Information Bureau (Cominform) was created, comprising the Soviet Union, Poland, Czechoslovakia, Hungary, Romania, Bulgaria, Yugoslavia, and the communist parties of France and Italy. The 'democratic' nations pledged to fight American 'imperialism'.

Meanwhile, the other European nations had accepted the British and French invitations to assemble at Paris in July 1947 to consider the Marshall Plan. The deliberate absence of the communist countries was not unwelcome to Ernest Bevin, who had initially feared that the Soviets would play the spoiling role of 'a Trojan horse' (Bartlett, 1984, p. 267). Within ten weeks a comprehensive scheme was drawn up for the economic recovery of Western Europe. In December Truman requested a congressional appropriation of $17 billion to fund the programme. Although the desire to help Europe was very evident, the Republican majority hesitated to grant such huge spending powers to a Democratic administration. However, doubts were dramatically dispelled by the communist coup in Czechoslovakia in February 1948, which sent shockwaves through Washington. 'Prompt passage' of the recovery programme, Truman informed Congress, 'is the most telling contribution we can now make toward peace'. The vote to implement the Marshall Plan was regarded as putting the 'Truman Doctrine in action'. The president solemnly concluded: 'We must be prepared to pay the price of peace, or assuredly we shall pay the price of war' (Schlesinger, 1983, I, pp. 128–9; Yergin, 1978, p. 321).

Historical Debate over the Origins of the Cold War

The Cold War has been the central issue of contemporary international affairs. Over several decades both sides have ritually denounced the other for causing the conflict. Denied open access to their own diplomatic archives, Soviet historians have faithfully adhered to their government's 'official' version of events. A much more diverse approach has been forthcoming from American historians, reflecting their country's pluralistic and open society. Indeed, historical investigation has been largely conducted by American historians with the result that an American perspective has dominated the literature and debate on the subject.

European scholars have generally acknowledged the subordinate roles played by their nations in the unfolding of the Cold War. Rather than accord special or unique significance to the Cold War, it has been regarded as yet another stage in the struggle for power and territory endemic in the history of modern Europe (Calvocoressi, 1982, p. 15). During the 1830s Alexis de Tocqueville predicted that the destiny of the world would ultimately fall under the sway of the

16

peoples of America and Russia (Halle, 1967, p. 10). In this sense the confrontation of the superpowers was inescapable. The United States was simply assuming the leadership of Western civilization against the forces of Eastern barbarianism.

Some American writers have seen the struggle as a straight-forward ideological battle of democracy versus communism, whose historical roots date back to 1917 (Fleming, 1961). Open hostility was evident as soon as the Bolshevists rose to power. President Woodrow Wilson publicly condemned the Bolshevist government and sent American troops to assist efforts to restore the imperial regime. The wartime partnership between Roosevelt and Stalin was therefore an aberration which derived solely from the mutual desire to defeat Nazi Germany. Rivalry resumed once this objective was achieved and was made even more acute by the fact that the war brought American and Soviet armies face to face in central Europe.

While not entirely ignoring the background of unfriendly relations, most historical investigation of the origins of the Cold War attaches crucial significance to the events of the mid-1940s. So fundamental was the change in the European balance of power that those particular years are regarded as marking a historical water-shed. The conventional view among American politicians and diplomats at the time was that the Soviet Union sought world domination. Stalin was accused of plotting a monolithic communist conspiracy, beginning with his refusal to allow free elections in Poland in contravention of the agreements made at Yalta. Communist control was imposed throughout Eastern Europe and probes were made against Iran, Turkey, and Greece. Western democracy was perceived to be in dire peril.

In 1919 the United States had withdrawn into isolationism, but in 1945 American policymakers were determined not to repeat what they regarded as an error which had directly contributed to the outbreak of the Second World War. As the world's richest nation, the United States possessed a special responsibility to assist those nations ravaged by the war. Initially, American diplomacy stressed the continuation of the wartime coalition and the fostering of international cooperation by means of the United Nations. But American officials were frustrated by Soviet non-cooperation. The policy of containment signified by the Truman Doctrine and the Marshall Plan was therefore a defensive act forced upon the United

States. This contemporary view that Stalin was responsible for the Cold War has been endorsed by many historians and represents the 'orthodox' American interpretation 'that the Cold War was the brave and essential response of free men to communist aggression' (Schlesinger, 1967, p. 23; Spanier, 1960; Feis, 1970).

The opposite conclusion was forthcoming from Soviet writers, who singled out American imperialism as the cause of the Cold War (Ponomaryov et al., 1974). Their analysis reflected an 'official' line which has scarcely altered since 1945. For example, Soviet news agencies criticized the Truman Doctrine only a day after it was enunciated as 'a smokescreen for expansion'. The United States government was believed to be under the control of 'Wall Street bosses', who sought to use American power to gain world economic supremacy. 'Alarmed by the achievements of Socialism in the U.S.S.R. . . . and by the post-war growth of the labour and democratic movements in all countries,' explained Andrei Zhadanov at the founding of the Cominform in 1947, 'the American reactionaries are disposed to take upon themselves the mission of "saviours" of the capitalist system from Communism' (Schlesinger, 1983, II, pp. 315, 353).

The partisan nature of the historical debate continued until the 1960s when it was enlivened by the emergence of the 'revisionist' school of American historians. Disillusionment with their government's justification of the Vietnam War combined with the opening of American diplomatic archives to bring into question many of the assumptions underlying the 'orthodox' view. Revisionists adopted a markedly sympathetic view of Soviet behaviour. They pointed out that Stalin had proved himself a reliable wartime ally of the United States. Attention was also drawn to the military and economic weakness of the Soviet Union in the late 1940s. So great was Soviet insecurity that there was understandable insistence on the establishment of friendly governments in neighbouring states. Stalin was motivated by caution rather than aggression. Indeed, the revisionists argue that American pressure provoked him into hostility and thereby precipitated the Cold War (Ambrose, 1983a; Horowitz, 1965).

The succession of Roosevelt by Truman in April 1945 is seen as especially significant by revisionists (Kolko, 1968; Williams, 1962). Whereas Roosevelt carefully cultivated a friendly personal relationship with Stalin, Truman blustered about, telling the Soviets to 'go to hell', and that agreements with them had been 'a one-way street' (Bernstein, 1970, p. 26). The language and actions of the Truman administration were unequivocally threatening to the Soviet Union. Economic pressure was applied by the sudden cancellation of Lend–Lease. Administration officials effectively frustrated Soviet hopes for financial aid in the form of German reparations or a large American loan (Kuklick, 1972). On the other hand, American assistance was liberally given to Greece and Turkey with the intention of establishing anti-communist governments on the very borders of the Soviet Union. One writer has even contended that Truman used the atomic bomb in 1945 not so much to defeat Japan, as to terrify the Soviets into making concessions to the United States (Alperovitz, 1965). The thrust of these arguments is that Truman must bear a heavy responsibility for starting the Cold War.

By concentrating on the importance of internal rather than external influences, the revisionists found themselves obliged to explain the dynamics of American foreign policy. Influenced by the Vietnam War and more than two decades of huge defence spending, one scholar has stressed the primacy of the 'national security state'. According to this view, the anti-Soviet prejudices of the State Department fused with the requirements of the military-industrial complex to propel the United States into what became a virtual war economy. The logical result was the state of Cold War with the Soviet Union (Yergin, 1978).

A similar and even more influential interpretation has stressed the significance of economic factors (Kolko, 1972; LaFeber, 1976; Williams, 1962). These historians have argued that American diplomacy has historically sought to serve the needs of American capitalism by seeking an 'open door' into overseas markets. In 1945 American officials were fearful of a recurrence of the Great Depression of the 1930s. They believed that American prosperity and even the survival of capitalism depended upon the creation of a liberal international economic order that would guarantee the principle of the 'open door'. This aim was fundamentally undermined by the creation of a Soviet 'closed' sphere of influence in Eastern Europe. The Truman administration therefore sought, although unsuccessfully, to secure Soviet compliance by exerting diplomatic and economic pressure.

19

Advocates of the 'orthodox' interpretation have complained that the revisionists adopted double standards (Maddox, 1973). While Stalin was granted legitimate national security needs which excused his actions no matter how aggressive, the United States was judged according to an impossible standard of virtuous international behaviour. It was also argued that revisionists have enjoyed the benefits of hindsight when they stressed Soviet weakness. Although the Red Army was reduced in total strength after 1945, recent research has revealed that this was not apparent to American officials at the time. American military experts acknowledged that the Soviet Union was incapable of launching a direct military attack on the United States, but they also predicted that the Soviets could speedily overrun a weak and unstable Western Europe (Leffler, 1984, pp. 359–64). Moreover, this anxiety was not just an American preoccupation. European leaders were also fearful of the Soviet threat. In 1946 Churchill had sought to alert American public opinion to the creation of the 'iron curtain' in Europe. Indeed, the British Foreign Office considered that State Department officials were too passive towards the Soviet Union (Anderson, 1981; Hathaway, 1981).

There has also been considerable controversy over whether Truman actually initiated a sharp break in American policy. Despite his desire for conciliation and compromise, Roosevelt deliberately refrained from informing Stalin of the American development of the atomic bomb. Annoyed by Stalin's refusal to broaden the composition of the Polish government, Roosevelt told Churchill only a few days before his death: 'We must not permit anybody to entertain a false impression that we are afraid. Our armies will in a very few days be in a position that will permit us to become "tougher" than has heretofore appeared advantageous to the war effort' (Dallek, 1979, p. 527). In contrast to his predecessor, Truman was inexperienced in foreign affairs and more receptive to the advice of anti-communist aides such as Ambassador Averell Harriman and Admiral Leahy. Nevertheless, his decision to send Harry Hopkins on a private mission to Moscow in May 1945 was reminiscent of Roosevelt's diplomacy and showed Truman's similar desire to seek agreement rather than confrontation with Stalin.

Furthermore, Truman was not simply a tool of military or

business interests. The military-industrial complex had grown enormously during the war, but its postwar ambitions were limited by political realities and the desire for demobilization within the United States itself. 'Atomic diplomacy' to coerce the Soviets was hardly feasible so long as the number of available atomic bombs was virtually nil (Sherwin, 1975). The Truman administration was certainly keen to promote exports and investment, but Eastern Europe was hardly one of their priorities in this respect. Moreover, the implementation of a grand economic design was severely constrained by domestic politics. Congress balked at granting a postwar loan to Britain, America's closest ally. Even the Marshall Plan was carefully scrutinized by congressmen who were more concerned with its actual costs rather than its possible benefits.

Despite the recent claim that a 'post-revisionist' synthesis has emerged among American historians, the historical controversy over the origins of the Cold War continues and is in danger of going around in circles (Gaddis, 1983; Leffler, 1984). If there has been any common ground, it is the agreement that American policymakers were acutely suspicious of the Soviet Union and irritated by her refusal to cooperate in making the postwar world over in the American image. The political vacuum in Europe made that continent the centre of attention and the focal point of superpower conflict. At this point historical interpretations sharply diverge. 'Orthodox' writers argue that Stalin was bent on world conquest and had to be resisted. Revisionists single out Truman as the instrument of economic forces and conclude that Stalin was a victim of unreasonable American pressure. The most recent research contends that both leaders pursued pragmatic policies. Stalin was cautious and averse to embarking upon another war, even though he was also keen to extend Soviet borders at the expense of the West. And while Truman was determined to resist communist aggression, his tough rhetoric disguised the lack of a coherent and systematic strategy. Indeed, the governments of Western Europe, especially Britain, were perturbed by what they regarded as American indifference towards the military threat posed by the Soviet Union in Europe (Frazier, 1984; Ovendale, 1982).

No matter which person, country, or system is held responsible, the historical fact is that the United States and the Soviet Union

21

had become adversaries by 1947. This relationship took on the peculiar state of 'cold' war in which both sides regularly heaped abuse upon the other and vigorously prepared for a third world war that never actually materialized.

2   Stalemate in Europe

The Berlin Blockade

In direct accordance with American intentions, the Marshall Plan provided a significant stimulus to the economies of the three Western zones in Germany. The Soviets were apprehensive and accused the United States not only of seeking to monopolize the economic resources of the Ruhr, but also of preparing for the creation of a West German political state. Fearful of the emergence of an anti-communist West Germany, the Soviets attempted to prevent this from happening by using the anomalous status of Berlin to make Germany the focus of international tension during 1948.

The ostensible basis of Soviet displeasure was their exclusion from Western deliberations on the future of Germany. Since the formation of Bizonia, the Western powers had pursued a unilateral course. The Allied Control Council was ignored in 1948 as they discussed among themselves the incorporation of the French zone and the drafting of a new constitution to permit a measure of German self-government. Moreover, in order to integrate the Western zones more fully into the Marshall Plan, the three powers also announced their intention to replace the greatly depreciated Reichsmark with the new Deutschmark. In retaliation at not being directly consulted, the Soviets formally withdrew from the Allied Control Council in March 1948. When the new currency was introduced into West Berlin in June, the Soviets declared that the Western powers had 'destroyed' the Four-power basis of governing Germany agreed on at Potsdam and had consequently forfeited 'the legal basis which assured their right to participate in the administration of Berlin' (Schlesinger, 1983, I, p. 483). On 24 June the Soviet authorities instituted a formal blockade by closing all road, rail, and water routes to and from the city. Shortly afterwards, the inhabitants of the Western sectors were cut off from all supplies of fuel, power, and food.

It was not surprising that Stalin should seek to make an issue over the city which Khrushchev later described as a bone in the Soviet throat. Smack in the middle of the Eastern zone, West Berlin represented a symbolic Western presence. To many thousands of refugees seeking to flee the drab Eastern sector, the Western sector appeared as a magnetic island of freedom. But its geographical isolation was also a decided weakness. Outnumbered and surrounded by the Red Army, the small Western garrison of 7,500 troops was placed in an untenable military position. Moreover, the Western rights of access to their sectors had never been exactly defined and were based on informal understandings made at the close of the war in 1945. The Soviet authorities had the power to cut the surface routes and to starve or even capture the Western garrisons whenever they might wish to do so. West Berlin was therefore a hostage to Soviet whims or designs and became the principal centre of Cold War tension in Europe.

The blockade caused consternation in the West, where it was interpreted as Soviet aggression calculated to force a Western withdrawal from Berlin. However, instead of a direct Soviet military attack, the Western powers had to contend with a challenge that was primarily political and psychological in nature. While resistance entailed the risk of unleashing a third world war, the alternative was to abandon the garrison and thereby place 2 million West Berliners under Soviet rule. Withdrawal had little appeal for American officials who considered that it would shatter Western prestige not only in Germany, but all over Europe.

Some believed, however, that Stalin was seeking to divert attention from his own difficulties with Tito in Yugoslavia and the failure of national strikes organized by communists in France and Italy. From his vantage point in Germany, General Clay advised a showdown. He was confident that the dispatch of an armed convoy along the autobahn would break the blockade and drive the Soviets into ignominious retreat: 'If we withdraw, our position in Europe is threatened. If America does not understand this now, does not know that the issue is cast, then it never will and communism will run rampant' (Clay, 1950, p. 361).

President Truman did not disagree. 'We are going to stay, period,' he characteristically asserted (Millis, 1951, p. 454). But fear of war ruled out Clay's recommendation to risk a military confrontation. The answer and eventual salvation for the city and its inhabitants was found in airlifting supplies. It was an extraordinary achievement in which each day thousands of tons of food and fuel were flown through a narrow air corridor into the beleaguered city. The West was able to compensate for its military inadequacy on the ground by demonstrating its superiority in the air. Moreover, the dilemma of whether or not to fire the first shot and thereby incur responsibility for initiating hostilities was ingeniously transferred to the Soviets.

Simultaneously, the Western authorities declared that the Soviet action was illegal, and instituted a counter-blockade against the Eastern zone. More ominously, a number of B-29 bombers capable of delivering atomic weapons were moved from the United States to Britain. The threat of the atmoic bomb was never made explicit because the Soviets were already effectively outmanoeuvred. Although they avoided interfering with the airlift, the Soviet authorities still appeared in the eyes of world opinion as ruthlessly seeking to starve millions of men, women, and children into submission. By contrast, the Western pilots were heroes and saviours.

On 12 May 1949 Stalin reopened all routes into the city. The blockade had lasted 324 days, during which the West had airlifted more than 1.5 million tons of supplies. Although its rights of access to Berlin still remained uncertain, the West claimed a victory in the first major confrontation of the superpowers in Europe. Far from undermining Western resolve, the blockade boosted morale and emphasized the close affinity of interests between Western Europe and the United States. The significance of airpower and resolute American leadership was vindicated. Moreover, instead of preventing the formation of a West German state, the crisis over Berlin actually accelerated the process by substantially strengthening anti-communism throughout Western Europe and especially in West Germany. In September 1949 the end of military rule in the three Western zones was signified by the establishment of the

German Federal Republic. Although West Berlin would be included in the new republic, the new capital was located at Bonn. In October Stalin responded by creating the German Democratic Republic. The end of the zonal system had resulted not in reunification, but the effective division of Germany into two separate and hostile countries.

Formation of NATO

Coming only a few months after the communist coup in Czechoslovakia, the Berlin crisis rekindled Western fears of communist aggression and directed attention to the urgent need for a Western military alliance. As early as March 1948 the governments of Britain, France, Belgium, Luxemburg, and the Netherlands had signed the Brussels Treaty to provide for mutual military assistance in the event of war. America's traditional aversion to entering into 'entangling alliances' meant, however, that the Truman administration remained aloof. Nevertheless, Truman welcomed the treaty in principle and was pleased to commend the development publicly. 'I am sure', he told Congress, 'that the determination of the free countries of Europe to protect themselves will be matched by an equal determination on our part to help them to do so' (Schlesinger, 1983, I, p. 128).

Rather than presidential statements of approval, the Western European governments wanted the formal commitment of American military power to defend Europe. Without the deterrent of American airpower and atomic weapons, they believed that there could be no security against communist aggression. The supreme commander of the Brussels Treaty forces, Field Marshal Montgomery, acknowledged that he was under instructions to defend the Rhine. 'With present forces', he lamented, 'I might be able to hold the tip of the Brittany Peninsula for 48 hours' (Achilles, 1985, p. 32). The Truman administration was sympathetic, but questioned whether Europe's defence required the United States to enter into a formal alliance in peacetime.

The passage in June 1948 of the Vandenberg Resolution by a large majority of the American Senate indicated, however, the existence of considerable bipartisan political support for some form of American 'association' with the Brussels Treaty (Schlesinger, 1983, I, p. 133). Congressmen were impressed by arguments stressing the natural affinities and common strategic interests between the two continents. They were keenly aware that the front line of their nation's defence was now the River Elbe and no longer the Atlantic shore. Also the crisis over Berlin was timely and instructive in demonstrating the vital importance of American leadership to counter aggression. Moreover, administration officials became increasingly fearful that European insecurity threatened to undermine the Marshall Plan. They considered that American military assistance was urgently required to enable the free nations of Europe to recover economically and politically. Otherwise, as Secretary of State Acheson warned, they would 'succumb one by one to the erosive and encroaching processes of Soviet expansion' (Graebner, 1984, p. 149).

For much of 1948 the Western governments engaged in prolonged and complex discussions at Washington in an attempt to define the exact nature of America's commitment. As the result of a British suggestion, the area to be offered protection was enlarged to comprise not only the United States and the countries of the Brussels Treaty, but also Canada, Scandinavia, and the Mediterranean. It was believed that this 'North Atlantic' region would be more strategically viable. By emphasizing the collective security aspect of the alliance, it would also be more politically acceptable to the parliaments of the member states.

A more difficult issue revolved around the desirability of a treaty. Despite the Vandenberg Resolution, it was known that several senators, including Vandenberg himself, preferred that their government confine itself to giving a single unilateral commitment similar to the Monroe Doctrine. Mindful of America's geographical position 3,000 miles away and her retreat into isolationism after the First World War, the Western European governments argued that a formal treaty containing a binding guarantee was essential to underline the long-term intention of the United States to defend Europe. 'France, on the outposts of Europe, cannot hold out alone,' stated the French prime minister, Henri Queuille. He added: 'If sufficient forces could be relied on to prevent the Russian army from crossing the Elbe, the civilisation of Europe would be safe. A fortnight after an invasion, it would be lost' (Delmas, 1985, p. 64).

27

American officials recognized the need for a treaty rather than a loose association. But considerable discussion ensued before they eventually conceded the guarantee contained in article five:

> The Parties agree that an armed attack against one or more of them in Europe or North America shall be considered an attack against them all; and ... if such an armed attack occurs, each of them ... will assist the Party or Parties so attacked by taking forthwith, individually and in concert with other Parties, such action as it deems necessary, including the use of armed force, to restore and maintain the security of the North Atlantic area. (Schlesinger, 1983, I, p. 141).

Despite the reference to collective action, the ultimate effectiveness of the alliance depended upon American military power. Consequently, the deliberate mention of 'the use of armed force' in article five pleased the European governments. Conscious, however, that only Congress could declare a state of war, the United States was careful to avoid giving an automatic commitment to go to war. Therefore, at American insistence, article 11 provided that implementation of the treaty must be in accordance with 'respective constitutional processes' (Schlesinger, 1983, I, p. 142). On 4 April 1949 the North Atlantic Treaty was signed in Washington by the United States, the five nations of the Brussels Treaty, Canada, Denmark, Iceland, Italy, Portugal, and Norway. Provision was made for regular meetings of the North Atlantic Council and the establishment of a permanent organization which would become known as NATO.

In July 1949 the American Senate ratified the treaty by a vote of 82 to 13. The debate revealed that Americans conceived of the alliance primarily as a psychological boost to a politically frightened and economically depressed Western Europe. In the immediate aftermath of Stalin's lifting of the Berlin blockade, there seemed no imminent likelihood of an all-out Soviet invasion of Western Europe. Therefore NATO could develop an initial strategy which was relatively inexpensive. A concept which soon gained popularity was that of the shield and the sword. Europe would provide the shield in the form of ground forces to halt a Soviet attack, while the sword was represented by the atomic weapons of America's Strategic

Air Command. Moreover, the military burden was scarcely a crushing one for the United States. The atomic bomb might never need to be used and would remain under independent American control. While two American divisions would continue to stay in Germany, there was no intention of dispatching additional American troops to replace European forces. Like the Marshall Plan, the Europeans were expected to assume the leading role in defending themselves.

This limited and defensive concept was soon altered by events. The discovery in August 1949 that the Soviets had successfully tested an atomic bomb dumbfounded American officials who had not expected such a development for at least another ten years. Furthermore, the passing of the atomic monopoly coincided with communist successes in China. The mood of anxiety prevailing in Washington was reflected in a comprehensive review of America's armed forces undertaken on behalf of the National Security Council. Known as NSC-68, this secret report was completed in April 1950. Starting with the premiss that the Soviet Union still actively sought world domination, NSC-68 argued that the military power of the United States was currently inadequate to prevent this. The report concluded that the United States must undertake an enormous military effort commensurate with wartime rearmament. It was unlikely, however, that Congress would readily agree to increasing the annual defence budget. But the timing of NSC-68 was fortuitous. The sudden outbreak of the Korean War in June 1950 confirmed the report's findings. The United States was plunged into a war on behalf of the United Nations against naked communist aggression. The anticipated congressional opposition was subdued and large defence appropriations were quickly secured. 'Korea came along and saved us,' Secretary of State Acheson later admitted (LaFeber, 1976, p. 100).

The invasion of South Korea had direct relevance for Europe since it raised the spectre of a similar communist attack against West Germany. The threat was made even more acute by the loss of America's atomic monopoly and the alarming imbalance in conventional forces between West and East. While the NATO countries could only put up to 14 divisions into the field in Europe, the Soviets were believed to possess at least 125 (Halle, 1967, p. 125). Imbued with a sense of crisis mixed with the crusading spirit

29

inherent in NSC-68, American policymakers considered that it was imperative to build up NATO's ground forces. But disharmony soon appeared within the alliance. The European governments lacked the economic resources of the United States. They were reluctant to rearm in peacetime and thereby damage their plans for much-needed economic revival. There was also awareness that the burden of building up costly and politically unpopular conventional forces was meant to fall primarily upon them rather than the United States. Furthermore, a move towards rearmament might even provoke a pre-emptive Soviet invasion.

In 1949 the United States had insisted on a North Atlantic treaty that was inherently flexible and left a wide latitude for future manoeuvre. A year later, in order to secure European agreement to rearm, the United States made her commitment to NATO more tangible and permanent. Acting to all intents and purposes like a European power, she now assumed the central military command of NATO's ground forces and promised to place additional troops in Europe. As a demonstration of American intentions, General Eisenhower was appointed supreme allied commander in Europe. From his headquarters in Paris he headed a unified command structure composed of balanced forces representing each of the member states. The protection of each and every ally was affirmed by the adoption of a 'forward strategy' which aimed at defending Europe as far to the east as possible.

The new strategy raised, however, the question of defending Germany. The formation of the Federal Republic in 1949 had been very much at America's instigation and was intended not only to gain a friend of the West, but also to establish a buffer against Soviet expansion. Nevertheless, while NATO included West Germany within its defensive plans, that country was not a member of the alliance and made no contribution to her own defence. The logic of incorporating German troops within NATO was conclusively accepted by the Truman administration, but Acheson's suggestion in September 1950 to raise ten German divisions only disconcerted the European allies. Embittered by the memory of three German invasions in less than a century, France was terrified of the prospect of a rearmed Germany. The French government grudgingly agreed to the principle of West German military participation in NATO only after the United States undertook to increase

30

military aid and to integrate American troops fully within NATO's command structure. In this way the Western European allies were partially compensated for bearing the costs of rearmament and given a guarantee of American protection against an invader, whether from the Soviet Union or Germany.

In January 1951 General Eisenhower returned to Europe, intent upon ensuring 'the survival of Western civilization' (Ambrose, 1983b, p. 496). He expressed confidence that the disparity in conventional forces between West and East would soon be redressed. Support was forthcoming from the members of NATO, who all pledged substantial increases in defence spending. The American Congress also agreed to send four extra divisions to Germany. Britain announced that she would retain military conscription. But a discordant note was sounded by George Kennan, who had once warned of the danger 'of a general preoccupation with military affairs, to the detriment of economic recovery and of the necessity for seeking a peaceful solution to Europe's difficulties' (Kennan, 1968, p. 410). His fears were fulfilled as the acceleration of the arms race between the superpowers resulted in an intensification of the Cold War.

Rearmament

'The North Atlantic pact', declared the Soviet Union in March 1949, 'is designed to daunt the states which do not agree to obey the dictates of the Anglo-American grouping of powers that lay claim to world domination' (Schlesinger, 1983, II, p. 404). The prospect of further military encirclement merely motivated Stalin to increase the strength of the Red Army from 2.8 million in 1948 to 5 million in 1953 (Ulam, 1973, p. 207). Additional resources were directed into weapons programmes that would ultimately lead to Soviet development of atomic and hydrogen bombs. Moreover, the spectre of German rearmament presented the Soviets with an extremely useful propaganda tool to call for continued sacrifices from their own people and those of the countries of Eastern Europe.

A Soviet empire of satellite states stretched from the Baltic to the Balkans. Although they nominally retained their independent identities, these countries were subordinated to Soviet political,

31

economic, and military direction. Obedience was ensured by the presence or the close proximity of the Red Army. Any tendency towards political dissent was ruthlessly eliminated so that no repetition of Tito's defection was allowed. Economic controls were imposed by the creation of the Council for Mutual Economic Assistance (COMECON) in 1949. Military affairs were also firmly under Soviet command. Training, the allocation of resources, and military planning were co-ordinated from Moscow. Even though the establishment of the Warsaw Pact was not publicly announced until 1955, a Soviet counterpart of NATO was already in existence.

In the United States, the desire to liberate Eastern Europe from communist tyranny became a prominent theme of Eisenhower's presidential-election campaign of 1952. The leading Republican spokesman on foreign affairs, John Foster Dulles, denounced the passivity of the Truman administration and declared that the United States must seize the initiative in the Cold War. Dulles fervently preached an 'end of the negative, futile and immoral policy of "containment" which abandons countless human beings to a despotism and Godless terrorism' (Halle, 1967, p. 270). The increasingly moralistic and uncompromising tone of Dulles towards the Soviet Union reflected not only the strategic imperatives of NSC-68, but also the prevailing American mood of paranoia associated with McCarthyism, the 'loss' of China, and the Korean War. The perception of communism as an evil that must be extirpated had a powerful political appeal and contributed to the election of Eisenhower in November 1952.

Eisenhower's victory led to the appointment of Dulles as secretary of state. Despite his tough campaign rhetoric, Dulles proved more circumspect in office. 'Rolling back' the Iron Curtain was still declared to be a priority. This would be achieved, however, not by force but by steadily exerting the superior moral and spiritual example of the 'free world' under the leadership of the United States. In any comparison between the two systems, Dulles claimed to speak from an unassailable position of strength. America was the most powerful economic country in the world and her wealth had fuelled an economic miracle in Western Europe. The contrast between the prosperous societies of Western Europe and the drab and impoverished people of the East was very marked. Further evidence of the triumph of democracy was the political decline of communist parties throughout the West. Communist rule was thoroughly discredited by its identification with purges, show trials, labour camps, and immense suffering. 'We know', Dulles stated, 'that the Soviet Communists' attempts to impose their absolute rule over 800 million captives involves them in what, in the long run, is an impossible task' (Gaddis, 1982, pp. 155–6).

Despite its wish for bold action against the Soviets, the new Republican administration had an even greater desire for a sound economy and a balanced budget. 'Our problem', observed Eisenhower, 'is to achieve military strength within the limits of endurable strain upon our economy' (Graebner, 1984, p. 194). Truman's policy of containment by rearmament was therefore discarded because the escalating financial burden must ultimately result in national bankruptcy. Instead, a strategy known as the 'new look' emerged which allowed a significant reduction of expensive conventional forces by placing increased emphasis on strategic airpower. While the air force would recruit an additional 30,000 men, the army would be reduced by 500,000. Nevertheless, America's destructive capacity would actually be enhanced by the acquisition of new airplanes and weapons systems giving 'more bang for the buck' (Divine, 1981, p. 37).

The 'new look' policy aroused apprehension in Western Europe that the United States was contemplating a return to isolationism. So close had been his military association with Europe, that Eisenhower expressed himself 'amazed' at this reaction. In his opinion, NATO remained the key to America's defence (Ambrose, 1984, pp. 33, 49). In 1952 the alliance had been extended to cover the eastern Mediterranean by the adhesion of Greece and Turkey. At the Lisbon council meeting of NATO in 1952 a goal of 96 divisions was set for 1954. The Eisenhower administration was particularly keen to see the European allies build up their ground forces in order to compensate for the proposed reduction in similar American forces. The target set at Lisbon was, however, so ambitious that its achievement would inevitably require the inclusion of substantial West German forces.

After the initial shock that greeted Acheson's proposal in 1950 to create a German army, the Western European governments gradually became reconciled to the military need for German rearmament. The main fear, especially in France, was the revival of

Germany as an independent military power. Signs of Franco-German *rapprochement* were indicated, however, by the inclusion of the German Federal Republic in the European Coal and Steel Community (ECSC) formed in 1951. At the instigation of the French government, a scheme was devised to create a multinational European army under NATO's command to which German units would be assigned. This integrated army was modelled on the ECSC and was known as the European Defence Community (EDC). A treaty to create the EDC was drawn up in 1952, but ratification encountered considerable resistance, particularly in the French National Assembly. Military experts questioned the feasibility of organizing an all-European army with a common uniform but different languages. Politicians argued that the concept encroached too far on national sovereignty.

As supreme commander of NATO, Eisenhower had constantly preached strength through unity. Ideally, he wished for a 'United States of Europe', which he believed would 'instantly ... solve the real and bitter problems of today' (Ambrose, 1983a, p. 508). Consequently, the Eisenhower administration was strongly in favour of the EDC, seeing it as the best possible spur towards the political unification of Europe. Dismayed by the protracted political debate in France, Dulles warned that rejection of the treaty would compel an 'agonizing reappraisal' of American policy towards Western Europe and the likelihood of a separate arrangement between Washington and Bonn (Graebner, 1984, p. 192).

Dulles's intervention, however, proved counter-productive. Already resentful of American criticism of her colonial policies in Algeria and Indo-China, France was keen to demonstrate that she was not a satellite of the United States. Consequently, her rejection of the EDC in August 1954 threw American diplomacy into disarray. But the need for German military integration within NATO was not in question, so ways were sought to resolve the apparent impasse. The atmosphere of gloom was lifted in October by the acceptance of a British initiative to include West Germany in an enlargement of the Brussels Treaty to be known as the Western European Union. Britain also announced that she would undertake to place four additional divisions in Germany. These gave the political and military reassurances required by the French government and paved the way for the acceptance of West Germany as a full member of NATO in 1955. Germany once more became an independent sovereign nation. In return, she agreed to restrict the size of her armed forces and pledged not to manufacture nuclear weapons, long-range missiles, or bombers.

The defeat of the EDC coincided with a slackening of defence spending by the NATO countries. Like the American taxpayer, Europeans were just as reluctant to see high military expenditures undermine their hopes of sustained economic growth. Rearmament was politically unpopular and held responsible for inflation and balance of payments difficulties. Countries such as Britain and France also found it impossible to give a priority to NATO when they faced pressing military commitments in their overseas colonial empires. Moreover, as the crises over the Berlin blockade and the outbreak of the Korean War receded into the past, there was less fear in Europe of imminent Soviet invasion.

The successful testing of the hydrogen bomb in 1952 and later deployment of nuclear weapons also brought into question the rationale for large standing armies. NATO's goal of 96 divisions proved excessively optimistic and was quickly reduced to 43. By 1954 only 25 divisions could be described as combat-ready (Osgood, 1962, p. 88). Even with German rearmament, it was clear that NATO's ground forces were inadequate to defend Europe from a full-scale Soviet attack. They could only hope to slow the aggressor's advance and thereby give time for the use of American strategic airpower. Western Europe's tacit reliance upon the latter had existed virtually since 1945, but Dulles gave it the new name of the strategy of 'massive retaliation'. 'We cannot build', he declared, 'a 20,000 mile Maginot Line or match the Red armies, man for man, gun for gun and tank for tank at any particular time or place their general staff selects' (Gaddis, 1982, p. 121). Instead, Dulles argued, the United States must use the 'deterrent of massive retaliatory power' and 'respond vigorously at places and with means of its own choosing' (Schlesinger, 1983, I, p. 230).

The European allies appreciated the advantages of substituting technology for conventional forces, but they were alarmed by the implications of 'massive retaliation'. They feared that the United States might transform a minor local conflict into a world war or, conversely, choose to back down rather than precipitate nuclear devastation. To insure against the latter contingency taking place on their own continent, they insisted that American troops remain in Germany as a visible guarantee of America's commitment to the defence of Europe. This function was described as a 'trip wire' or 'plate glass window'. Moreover, if NATO's troops were unable to defend Europe, they must still provide a credible capacity to deter aggression. Consequently, it was decided in 1954 to compensate for the lack of conventional forces by deploying tactical nuclear weapons under American command. The use of low-yield nuclear weapons would, however, be restricted to the immediate battle zone. 'We have determined that our strategy in the center requires the use of atomic weapons, whether the enemy uses them or not,' stated General Gruenther in 1954. The supreme allied commander added: 'We must use atomic bombs to redress the imbalance between their forces and ours to achieve victory' (Osgood, 1962, p. 109). Technological advance brought tangible economic benefits, but it also introduced a balance of terror in which war posed the appalling prospect of annihilation.

If the threat of nuclear holocaust deterred a Soviet invasion of Western Europe, it also effectively prevented the United States from rolling back the Iron Curtain. Despite Soviet political weakness after the death of Stalin in 1953, the new leaders of the Kremlin were determined to maintain control over Eastern Europe. Disturbances in East Germany in 1953 and Poland in 1956 were quickly quelled. When a major revolt occurred in Hungary in 1956, it was ruthlessly suppressed by Soviet tanks. Dulles praised the patriotism of the rebels and led the condemnation of Soviet brutality at the United Nations. But his attitude of moral superiority rang hollow in the face of tanks on the streets of Budapest. Eisenhower privately admitted that the use of atomic weapons was an option. 'But to annihilate Hungary', he despairingly concluded, 'is in no way to help her' (Ambrose, 1984, p. 372). Despite the stress on rearmament and acquiring a position of military strength, the Eisenhower administration was unwilling to intervene militarily. In effect, the United States tacitly acknowledged that Eastern Europe was a Soviet sphere of influence.

Decline of the Cold War in Europe

While the Soviets remained impervious to American criticism of

36

their stranglehold over Eastern Europe, a more amenable diplomatic approach towards the West was evident in other matters. The death of Stalin in March 1953 afforded an opportunity to ease tensions. 'We are not angry with anybody,' stressed the new Soviet premier, Georgi Malenkov (Ulam, 1973, p. 208). Churchill suggested an immediate 'summit' meeting, but Dulles was highly suspicious of Malenkov's 'phony peace campaign' (Divine, 1981, p. 109). Nevertheless, aggressive actions such as the blockade of Berlin were not repeated. Instead, Soviet diplomatic influence was exerted to bring about an armistice in Korea in 1953. Proposals also emanated from Moscow for Four-power agreement to end the military occupation of Germany by creating a unified and neutral country. Although the German question remained unresolved, a similar scheme was acceptable in the case of Austria. Indeed, the signing of the Austrian Treaty in 1955 raised hopes of a 'thaw' in the Cold War and enabled President Eisenhower to propose a summit meeting to 'change the spirit' of relations between the superpowers (Ambrose, 1984, p. 261).

For the first time since the Potsdam conference ten years earlier, the leaders of the great powers met together at Geneva in July 1955. The agenda covered many subjects ranging from disarmament to Germany. The talks, however, were inconclusive and the powers simply agreed to disagree. 'They drank little and smiled much,' was how Eisenhower summed up the behaviour of the Soviet leaders, Bulganin and Khrushchev (Divine, 1981, p. 119). The president also mentioned that each side 'intended to pursue a new spirit of conciliation and cooperation in its contacts with the other' (Ambrose, 1984, p. 267). This optimism was, however, sorely tested by the suppression of the Hungarian uprising during 1956.

Emboldened by the West's passivity during the Hungarian crisis, Soviet diplomacy subsequently assumed a more aggressive and challenging tone. Indeed, the West faced a formidable antagonist in Nikita Khrushchev, who finally achieved political supremacy over his rivals in 1957. By denouncing Stalin's 'cult of personality' at the 20th Party Congress in 1956, Khrushchev gave an impetus and enhanced respectability to world communism. The boasts did not go unheeded, for Khrushchev represented a nation which now possessed its own growing arsenal of nuclear weapons. Moreover, in October 1957 the Soviet Union delivered an enormous psychological blow to American pride by sending the sputnik round the earth. The age of the intercontinental ballistic missile was thereby inaugurated. In what he saw as the intensification of the struggle for 'peaceful co-existence', Khrushchev asserted that the economic and scientific progress of communist countries would defeat the West without resorting to war.

The test of strength in Europe came in Berlin. Still a thorn in the Soviet side, the Western sectors had enjoyed spectacular prosperity since 1949. During the ensuing decade, almost two million East German refugees used the city to escape to the West. Suddenly in November 1958, Khrushchev created an international crisis by demanding an end to the 'unlawful occupation of West Berlin'. Instead of imposing a military blockade, he adopted the tactics of psychological warfare. If the Western garrisons were not withdrawn from the city within six months, the Soviets threatened to sign a separate peace treaty with East Germany which would place all the access routes under the latter's control (Schlesinger, 1983, II, pp. 600–4). Such an outcome would be unacceptable to the Western powers since they did not recognize East Germany. To ignore Khrushchev's ultimatum, however, would entail the risk of nuclear war.

Eisenhower regarded Khrushchev's action as part of a Soviet strategy calculated to probe the West's most vulnerable spots. 'They would like us to go frantic every time they stir up difficulties in these areas,' he noted (Ambrose, 1984, p. 520). Nevertheless, the president believed that the United States had a 'solemn obligation' to defend the citizens of West Berlin (Divine, 1981, p. 133). Although he was determined to stand firm, Eisenhower wished to avoid war. Subsequent diplomatic events demonstrated that Khrushchev also sought conciliation rather than confrontation. When the British prime minister, Harold Macmillan, visited Moscow in March 1959, he was told that the Soviets would call off the deadline if a summit meeting was arranged. Eisenhower countered by insisting that a preliminary meeting of foreign ministers be held first at Geneva. Khrushchev agreed and quietly abandoned the original deadline. The foreign ministers met at Geneva in May and Khrushchev visited the United States in September. A summit meeting was eventually arranged at Paris in May 1960, but any chance of substantive discussions was rendered abortive by the shooting down of a U-2 American reconnaissance plane over the Soviet Union.

Thwarted over Berlin, Khrushchev used Eisenhower's belated admission of having known of the U-2 flights as a propaganda club with which to humiliate the United States. The Soviet defence minister, Marshal Malinovsky, ominously warned that his country possessed the weapons to strike 'both at the satellites and at the leader' of the Western alliance, 'no matter what seas and oceans they may hide behind' (Halle, 1967, p. 375). But Soviet aggressiveness only gave further alarm to the West and stimulated another round of the arms race. Since the launch of Sputnik in 1957, American military experts had claimed that the Soviets enjoyed such a decisive superiority in missile technology that they would soon be able to launch a devastating 'first strike' upon the United States. This fear was successfully exploited in the 1960 presidential-election campaign by John F. Kennedy, who charged that the Eisenhower administration had allowed the creation of a 'missile gap'. On assuming the presidency in 1961, Kennedy signalled his intentions by requesting Congress to increase annual defence spending by an extra $6 billion.

The new president also sought a personal meeting with Khrushchev. This took place at Vienna in June 1961. Khrushchev tried to bully the younger man and renewed the Berlin crisis by threatening to sign a peace treaty with East Germany. As the two leaders parted, Kennedy said: 'It's going to be a cold winter' (Salinger, 1967, p. 182). Some weeks later, Kennedy stated on national television that West Berlin 'has now become, as never before, the great testing place of Western courage and will' (Schlesinger, 1983, I, p. 665). Simultaneously, the president announced his decision to call up 150,000 army reservists and to increase the size of NATO's ground forces. Kennedy warned: 'We cannot and will not permit the Communists to drive us out of Berlin, either gradually or by force' (1983, I, p. 665).

In West Berlin, each day saw the arrival of more than one thousand East German refugees. Quite unexpectedly, the East German authorities erected a barbed-wire fence during the night of 12–13 August 1961. The fence soon became the notorious Berlin Wall, separating the Eastern and Western sectors. The West seized its opportunity to condemn a society which had to build a wall to keep its own people captive. The Soviets countered by describing West Berlin as a den of 'international criminals and provocateurs of all kinds' (Schlesinger, 1983, I, p. 672). The diplomatic dialogue was heated, but there was no disposition to resort to force. The Berlin crisis was allowed to fade away as both sides acknowledged that the partition of Germany was an undeniable fact. The Wall therefore achieved Khrushchev's purpose of halting the flood of refugees and gave valuable breathing space to the communist rulers of the German Democratic Republic. On the other hand, West Germany was confirmed as a fully integrated member of the Western alliance.

The balance of nuclear weaponry was also swinging decisively against the Soviet Union. There was, in fact, no missile gap. Even before Kennedy took office, the United States had developed Polaris submarines and Atlas missiles. American superiority in strategic weapons was further underlined in 1962 by the deployment of Titan and Minuteman missiles. The United States appeared to have a 'first strike' capability and was forging even further ahead. Khrushchev secretly attempted to redress the strategic balance by placing missiles in Cuba. Once installed, these weapons would provide the Soviets with the means to destroy most of the eastern seaboard of the United States.

In October 1962 American U-2 reconnaissance flights revealed that missile sites were under construction in Cuba. A shocked Kennedy hastily convened his advisers. The president was determined to avoid a show of weakness, but he was fearful of starting off a nuclear war. Amongst his advisers, the 'hawks' recommended air strikes to destroy the missile bases, while the 'doves' advocated a diplomatic solution. It was known, however, that most of the Soviet military equipment was still at sea *en route* to Cuba. Kennedy favoured therefore the establishment of a naval blockade to prevent this equipment from reaching its destination. It was a calculated decision that indicated American firmness and also allowed Khrushchev time to consider his reply.

On 22 October Kennedy appeared on television to inform the American people of Khrushchev's 'clandestine, reckless and provocative threat to world peace' (Schlesinger, 1983, III, p. 595). A sombre mood prevailed in Washington where American officials were worried that the Soviets might attempt to break the blockade or create a diversion over Berlin. The world was poised on the edge of nuclear disaster as the two superpowers engaged in an eyeball-to-eyeball confrontation. On 28 October Khrushchev agreed to dismantle the bases. Soviet ships *en route* to Cuba were turned around. In return, Kennedy gave assurances that the United States would not invade the island.

It seemed that Kennedy's firmness had forced Khrushchev to climb down. But the president had no desire to humiliate his adversary. He tactfully welcomed Khrushchev's message of 28 October and described it as 'an important contribution to peace' (Schlesinger, 1983, III, p. 606). Both leaders were chastened by the experience of being taken to the brink of nuclear war. In a celebrated speech delivered at the American University in June 1963, Kennedy stated:

> Let us examine our attitude toward the Cold War, remembering that we are not engaged in a debate, seeking to pile up debating points. We are not here distributing blame or pointing the finger of judgment. We must deal with the world as it is, and not as it might have been had the history of the last eighteen years been different. (Walton, 1973, p. 151)

Khrushchev later complimented Kennedy on 'the greatest speech by an American President since Roosevelt' (Schlesinger, 1965, p. 772). Symbolic of the changed mood was the setting up of a direct 'hotline' between Moscow and Washington in 1963. After years of fruitless discussion, agreement was also reached in July 1963 on a Nuclear Test Ban Treaty to outlaw atmospheric tests. Kennedy noted that 'While it will not end the threat of nuclear war,' the treaty 'can reduce tensions, open a way to further agreements, and thereby help to ease the threat of war' (Schlesinger, 1983, II, p. 731).

The European members of NATO reacted ambivalently to the signs of *détente* between the superpowers. The development of massive Soviet nuclear forces had only made Western Europe more dependent on the American nuclear deterrent. Notably, President Charles de Gaulle of France argued that the defence of Europe had become a secondary consideration for the United States. Since America was now also in danger of a direct attack from long-range Soviet missiles, he questioned whether the United States would risk a nuclear exchange that might result in her own national extinction.

De Gaulle also cited the example of the Cuban missile crisis, in which, he claimed, Kennedy had been prepared to precipitate a nuclear war without consulting his allies. Consequently, de Gaulle sought an independent nuclear force for France and pointedly refused to join the Test Ban Treaty (Schlesinger, 1983, I, p. 834).

The French president's independent stance reflected not only his strong personality, but also the re-emergence of European prestige and influence. Since the dark days of the late 1940s, Western Europe had achieved spectacular economic growth and political stability. Under the impetus of the European Economic Community (EEC) formed in 1955, Western Europe was fast acquiring a new sense of identity and self-esteem. In a striking reversal of historic tradition, Britain applied for admission to the EEC in 1962. But de Gaulle vetoed British membership. In his opinion, the application was part of a plot to extend America's control of NATO to the EEC. A mood of anti-Americanism was evident throughout Western Europe during the 1960s, but no government was willing to imitate de Gaulle's example of 1966 by withdrawing their forces assigned to NATO. Nevertheless, while the countries of Western Europe continued to regard NATO as fundamental to their security, they were no longer so terrified of a Soviet invasion and wished to improve relations with the countries of the Eastern bloc.

Accustomed to unquestioned predominance in NATO, American officials were understandably surprised, if not irritated, by Europe's desire and capacity to assert its independence of action. Both Kennedy and Johnson were eager that the European allies should concentrate on building up their conventional forces. They contended that those governments were content to shelter under America's nuclear umbrella while doing too little to protect themselves. The argument was familiar, but the imperatives for action had changed by the beginning of the 1960s. More than a decade of peace and prosperity had bolstered Western Europe's self-confidence and sense of security. Despite the presence of enormous military forces facing each other in central Europe, the prospect of mutually assured destruction (MAD) made war increasingly 'unthinkable'. Moreover, the frightening spectre of a monolithic communist conspiracy had been removed by the revelation of the Sino-Soviet split. The Cold War was hardly at an end, but Europeans regarded it as in decline. Indeed, as de Gaulle argued, the focal point of the struggle had demonstrably moved from Europe to Asia. While the images and language of the Cold War originated from the conflict between West and East over postwar Europe, the real military battles were actually taking place elsewhere.

3   Quagmire in Asia

The China Tangle

For more than a thousand years the vast Chinese empire exercised
dominion over the countries of the Far East. However, during the
nineteenth century, China's superior status was rudely challenged
and diminished by the European powers. The 1911 revolution
ended the empire, but the new republic failed to achieve political
and economic stability. Preoccupied with their own internal affairs,
the nations of Europe were unable to exploit China's weakness.
Consequently, Japan was the main beneficiary. Dating from her
victory over tsarist Russia in 1904–5, Japan steadily extended her
influence and possessions on the Asian mainland. Her attack on
Manchuria in 1931 widened six years later into full-scale war with
China and was part of a strategy designed to establish the 'Greater
East Asia Co-Prosperity Sphere'. But Japanese dreams of he-
gemony eventually provoked the direct military intervention of the
United States.

   Although her ties with Europe were much stronger and more
influential, the United States also bordered the Pacific Ocean and
consequently looked westwards to Asia. Her emerging commercial
and strategic interests in this region were underlined by the
acquisition of the Hawaiian and Philippine islands in 1898–9. The
United States developed a particularly friendly relationship with
China. A policy known as the 'open door' was pursued in which
American merchants gained equal access to the vast China market
in return for their government's pledge to uphold China's territorial
integrity and political independence. Within the United States, a
'China lobby' emerged to advocate closer political and economic

ties. Indeed, the American public needed little persuasion, for it manifested a genuine sympathy for the Chinese people in their struggle against European and Japanese imperialism. However, the desire to act as the self-appointed protector of China inevitably resulted in strained relations between the United States and Japan, culminating in the latter's pre-emptive assault on Pearl Harbor in 1941.

Despite the public demand for revenge against Japan, the Roosevelt administration insisted on following a Europe-first strategy during the Second World War. American troops were sent to fight in Europe, but not on the Asian mainland. Instead, the United States preferred to mobilize her enormous air and naval power in a gradual island-hopping campaign across the Pacific. But Japanese resistance was fierce and fanatical. Consequently, the maintenance of a second military front in China became an important element of Roosevelt's Far Eastern strategy. American financial and military support was given to the nationalist government of Chiang Kai-shek (Jiang Jieshi) so that it could continue the war and thereby tie down large numbers of Japanese forces on the mainland. For the same reason, Roosevelt was eager to persuade Stalin to enter the war against Japan in August 1945.

Instead of a massive invasion of the Japanese home islands, the dropping of the atomic bombs in August 1945 brought an unexpectedly sudden Japanese surrender. Japan's defeat was total and confirmed that the United States was indisputably the predominant power in the region. An allied council consisting of the United States, the British Commonwealth, China and the Soviet Union was established at Tokyo. President Truman insisted, however, that the council possessed only an advisory function. In contrast to the allied disagreement which emerged over Germany's role in Europe, Japan was not allowed to become a contentious issue in Asia. Indeed, the United States pointedly refused to allow the Soviets to participate in the military occupation of Japan. The post of supreme commander was assigned to General Douglas MacArthur. With characteristic American idealism, MacArthur declared his intention to convert Japan into 'the world's greatest laboratory for an experiment in the liberation of a people from totalitarian military rule and for the liberalization of government from within' (Manchester, 1979, pp. 429–30). Soviet protests went unheeded as

MacArthur proceeded to exercise autocratic control over a defeated nation which was to be disarmed and reformed according to American dictates.

Despite the controversy surrounding MacArthur's style of governing Japan, American diplomats were more interested in the postwar future of China. 'Americans', remarked George Kennan, 'tended to exaggerate China's real importance and to underrate that of Japan' (Kennan, 1968, p. 374). By restraining Japan, American diplomacy sought to alter the balance of power in the region so that China would resume an important geographical role. During the Second World War, Roosevelt had always insisted that China should be treated as a great power. Although he became increasingly disappointed with her actual military contribution to the war effort, Roosevelt held fast to the idea that China would act as one of the world's 'four policemen', helping to maintain the postwar peace. The president declared that for more than a century the Chinese people 'have been, in thought and in objective, closer to us Americans than almost any other peoples in the world' (Dallek, 1979, p. 391). In his opinion, a strong and democratic China would speed the advance of economic and political progress throughout the Far East. This favourable image, however, sharply diverged from the reality of a country divided by civil war.

The Kuomintang (Guomindang), or Nationalist party, had ruled China since the 1920s. The United States officially recognized the nationalist government in 1928 and entered into alliance with it in the war against Japan. The nationalist leader, Chiang Kai-shek, was particularly admired in the United States, where the China lobby praised his efforts to defend freedom against the evil fascist Japan. Moreover, Chiang's conversion to Christianity and the fact that his wife had been educated in the United States further enhanced his image as a champion of Western values. On the other hand, the nationalists were known to be notoriously corrupt and inefficient. They were dominated by a military clique whose oppressive rule aroused increasing unrest and provoked a major agrarian revolt led by the communist party under Mao Tse-tung (Mao Zedong). Roosevelt was only too well aware of the dangers of becoming ensnared in the tangle of Chinese politics, but he believed that it was essential to maintain Chiang in power if China was to remain in the war. The alternatives of political chaos or a communist regime were unacceptable.

46

At the close of the war with Japan, Soviet troops entered Manchuria in accordance with the wartime agreement made at Yalta by Roosevelt and Stalin. In China herself, Mao controlled large areas of the north and boasted an army of 500,000 men. The prospect of further communist advances prompted the Truman administration to despatch 50,000 American marines to help the nationalists repatriate the Japanese forces and re-establish their authority in the important cities of east China. But Chiang's hold on power was extremely precarious. American officials feared the outbreak of a full-scale civil war and sought to avoid this by encouraging the creation of a coalition government. They believed that the nationalists and communists had co-operated in the past and could do so again.

General Marshall was sent to China with the task of bringing Chiang and Mao together. Although a ceasefire was forthcoming in December 1945, this proved an empty gesture since the nationalists and communists thoroughly distrusted each other and were not disposed to negotiate a Western-style political compromise. The futility of Marshall's attempted mediation and the limits of American influence were underlined by Chiang's unilateral decision to launch a military offensive against the communists in the northeast. In January 1947 Marshall confessed defeat and complained of the 'almost insurmountable and maddening obstacles to bring some measure of peace to China' (Schlesinger, 1983, IV, p. 125).

American officials believed that Chiang had seriously blundered in renewing the civil war. Acheson described the offensive as 'the death wish of the Kuomintang' (Acheson, 1970, p. 203). By 1947, however, China had become a matter of less urgency for American diplomacy. The Soviet menace had markedly receded when Soviet troops were pulled out of Manchuria in the spring of 1946. In fact, Stalin adhered to the peace treaty which he had signed with Chiang in August 1945 and continued to recognize the nationalists as the official government of China. Despite the apparent ideological affinity between Mao and Stalin, Soviet influence was not overtly visible in Chinese affairs. 'There is a good chance', argued George Kennan, 'that if you let the Russians alone in China they will come a cropper on that problem just as everybody else has for hundreds of years' (Kennan, 1968, p. 374).

The Truman administration wished to extricate itself from the

47

China tangle. American marines were withdrawn during 1947 to avoid any possibility of their becoming directly involved in the civil war. A complication was raised, however, by Chiang's skill in mobilizing the support of the China lobby in Washington. Posing as the 'co-defender of democracy', Chiang astutely appealed for American aid 'against the onrush and infiltration of Communism throughout the world' (Schlesinger, 1983, IV, p. 155). While the Truman administration dared not 'abandon' Chiang, it would only grant him limited assistance. To defeat the Chinese communists, Marshall explained, 'it would be necessary for the United States virtually to take over the Chinese Government and administer its economic, military and governmental affairs' (Schlesinger, 1983, IV, p. 154). The idea of such a massive American commitment had always been rejected. Moreover, the stark reality of China's economic and political chaos removed the pretence that the country warranted great power status. Since China could not conceivably be considered a military threat to the United States, the Far East was downgraded in strategic importance. American officials directed their attention to what they considered to be the much more pressing threat of communism in Europe.

In 1949, however, the military stalemate was dramatically broken. The communists advanced from their base in Manchuria and overran the mainland. In September 1949 Mao established the People's Republic. By the end of the year, Chiang had retreated to the island of Formosa (Taiwan). The Truman administration was confounded by the turn of events, but not altogether surprised. American officials were instructed to remain in China and it seemed that diplomatic relations might be established with the new regime. In August Secretary of State Acheson sought to explain American policy by releasing a selection of important documents known as the *China White Paper*. In his opinion:

> The unfortunate but inescapable fact is that the ominous result of the civil war in China was beyond the control of the government of the United States. Nothing that this country did or could have done within the reasonable limits of its capabilities could have changed that result; nothing that was left undone by this country has contributed to it. It was the product of internal Chinese forces, forces which this

country tried to influence but could not. (Acheson, 1970, p. 303)

Acheson later recalled that the *China White Paper* was greeted 'by a storm of abuse from very diverse groups in the Congress and the press' (Acheson, 1970, p. 303). Critics were disturbed and infuriated by the implication that the United States had been incapable of preventing Chiang's downfall. They also pointed out that Acheson's complacent acceptance of the primacy of 'internal Chinese forces' was a direct acknowledgement of communist supremacy. One group of American senators issued a public statement condemning the document as a '1,054 page whitewash of a wishful, do-nothing policy which has succeeded in placing Asia in danger of Soviet conquest with its ultimate threat to the peace of the world and of our own national security' (Graebner, 1984, p. 169).

The timing of the document was unfortunate for the administration in coming so soon after the war scare over the Berlin blockade. It also coincided with the formation of NATO and the news of the Soviet explosion of an atomic bomb. Consequently, many Americans readily attached a global significance to the events in China. Rather than an indigenous rising against an oppressive and corrupt regime, the communist victory was interpreted as part of a world conspiracy directed from Moscow. The Chinese communist leaders were merely tools who obediently served the interests of Soviet imperialism. This was apparently confirmed by Mao's visit to Moscow in December 1949, followed by the signing of the Sino-Soviet treaty of alliance in February 1950.

Republican critics joined with the China lobby to berate the administration for doing too little for Chiang and therefore 'losing' China. But there was not only incompetence to blame. The Truman administration was accused of assuming a cowardly direction because it contained traitors who manipulated policy in the interests of the Soviet Union. Fear of infiltration by 'reds' had already prompted investigations of 'loyalty' and 'un-American activities'. The mood turned to national paranoia when the theme was taken up by Senator Joe McCarthy of Wisconsin. In a speech at Wheeling, West Virginia in February 1950, McCarthy claimed that he possessed the names of known communists who were currently working in the State Department. The upsurge of McCarthyism transformed the 'loss' of China into a powerful and emotive political issue. The question of recognizing the new regime was abruptly dumped as American officials sought to prove that they had never been nor would they ever be 'soft' on communism. In the process, China became an integral element in the Cold War struggle between the superpowers.

The Korean War

Surrounded by powerful neighbours, the people of the Korean peninsula were long accustomed to external interference in their affairs. At the turn of the twentieth century, control of the region was fiercely contested between China, Russia, and Japan. The latter was ultimately victorious and incorporated Korea within the Japanese empire from 1910 until 1945. The United States tacitly acquiesced in Japan's ascendancy and showed little interest in Korea until the Second World War. Because it was one of the victims of Japanese aggression, Roosevelt believed that Korea should become independent at the end of the war. But no discussion was undertaken as to how this might be implemented. After Japan's surrender in 1945, Soviet troops crossed into Korea from neighbouring Siberia. The United States was militarily unprepared, but wished to prevent the Soviet Union from absorbing the whole of Korea by default. American troops were therefore airlifted to the south and a dividing line between the two armies was arbitrarily drawn at the 38th parallel.

Both the United States and the Soviet Union affirmed their aim of establishing a united and independent Korea. A mutual withdrawal of the occupying forces was agreed, although this was not fully implemented until 1949. So intractable were the internal divisions within Korea, that it proved impossible to unify the country either by means of a trustee system or national elections supervised by the United Nations. Consequently, the temporary dividing line of the 38th parallel became permanent and separated the country into two antagonistic rival states. In the north, the communists were dominant and formed the Democratic People's Republic of Korea. Its leader was the Marxist revolutionary, Kim Il-sung, who had spent the Second World War in the Soviet Union.

In marked contrast, the southern leader, Syngman Rhee, had lived in America for more than 30 years. Although Rhee was a staunch nationalist, he closely aligned the Republic of Korea with the United States. The tensions of the Cold War were replicated in Korea as Kim and Rhee vilified each other for causing the division of the country. Both leaders declared that they would bring about reunification by whatever means were necessary, including the use of force.

In January 1950 the Korean question became entwined with that of China. Responding to public anxiety over American intentions towards Taiwan, President Truman informed the press that the United States had no intention of interfering militarily to protect Chiang. A week later in a celebrated speech delivered at the Washington Press Club, Secretary of State Acheson sought to clarify the president's remarks by stating that American strategy in the Far East was unchanged. He stressed that America's military power depended upon maintaining a string of naval and air bases running from the Aleutians to Japan, the Ryukyus, and the Philippines. These islands formed the nation's front line of defence. By implication, other countries such as Taiwan and South Korea lay outside what was described as America's 'defensive perimeter' (Schlesinger, 1983, IV, p. 362).

Although Roosevelt and Truman had supplied Chiang with financial aid, they had never been willing to fight to ensure his political survival. After Acheson's speech, it looked as if the United States would not contest an invasion of Taiwan by the Chinese communists. America was searching its soul over the 'loss' of China and the tide was clearly turning in favour of the communists. The expected hostilities erupted, however, not in Taiwan, but in Korea, where Kim Il-sung had carefully prepared his army and air force for a major offensive. With the apparent approval of the Soviet Union, he ordered his forces to invade South Korea on 25 June 1950.

Stalin and Kim had good reason to believe that the United States would remain passive. The Truman administration, however, chose to reverse its policy of military disengagement from the Asian mainland. Kim's initiative was not attributed to internal Korean politics. Under the influence of McCarthyism and the warnings of communist conspiracy contained in NSC-68, American officials were convinced that the Soviets had planned the invasion to test the resolve of the West. On receiving news of the crisis by telephone, Truman immediately flew from Missouri to Washington. He later recalled:

> I had time to think aboard the plane. In my generation, this was not the first occasion when the strong had attacked the weak. I recalled some earlier instances: Manchuria, Ethiopia, Austria. I remembered how each time that the democracies failed to act it had encouraged the aggressors to keep going ahead. Communism was acting in Korea just as Hitler, Mussolini, and the Japanese had acted ten, fifteen, and twenty years earlier... If this was allowed to go unchallenged it would mean a third world war, just as similar incidents had brought on a second world war. (Truman, 1956, p. 351)

Truman placed events in an international perspective. He was determined that there should be no repetition of appeasement. 'This is the Greece of the Far East,' the president told his staff (May, 1973, p. 71). The defence of South Korea was now considered vital to America's national security. But there was no NATO or military alliance that South Korea could invoke. Since the United States was not under attack, the American Congress could hardly declare a state of war. Truman therefore requested an immediate meeting of the Security Council of the United Nations. Assisted by the fortuitous absence of the Soviet representative, the American delegation secured the unanimous passage of a resolution calling upon North Korea to withdraw. A second resolution was passed two days later asking members of the United Nations to provide troops to drive back the invaders. On 27 June Truman announced that the United States would comply with the resolution and deploy her military forces on behalf of the United Nations. In reality, it was an 'American' war. Although 16 nations eventually sent troops, the American contribution was so much the largest that the various contingents were unified under American control and direction. General MacArthur was transferred from Japan to assume command.

During the first weeks of fighting, the North Koreans virtually overran the whole peninsula. In September, however, MacArthur brilliantly outflanked the enemy by making an amphibious landing at Inchon. With the North Koreans in headlong retreat, the United Nations (UN) forces crossed the 38th parallel and steadily advanced to the Yalu river, which marked the North Korean border with China. MacArthur had predicted that neither the Soviets nor China would join the war, but he was proved wrong in November when China launched the first of two major offensives. It was now the turn of the UN troops to retreat. The lines of battle moved back and forth until both sides consolidated their positions close to the 38th parallel.

In the meantime, MacArthur clashed with Truman over military tactics and was removed for exceeding his instructions. The president refused to expand the war beyond Korea and ruled out retaliatory air strikes against China. Truman's caution had already been demonstrated earlier in December 1950, when he responded to the appeals of the British prime minister, Clement Attlee, to withdraw the veiled threat to use atomic weapons. Moreover, by halting the UN forces at the 38th parallel, Truman indicated that he was willing to accept the prewar status quo. The strategy of 'limited' war resulted, however, in a military stalemate that proved not only costly in casualties, but also an increasing political liability for the Truman administration. Dwight Eisenhower correctly perceived the growing disenchantment of American public opinion. His campaign pledge 'to go to Korea' had an amazing impact and contributed significantly to his election in November 1952. Shortly after assuming office, Eisenhower issued a veiled threat to use atomic weapons against China. This threat combined with the evident war-weariness on both sides to bring about a ceasefire signed at Panmunjom in July 1953. Although provision was made for future conferences to discuss reunification, the politics of the Cold War ensured that the peninsula would remain divided at the 38th parallel. North Korea stayed firmly within the communist orbit, while South Korea became closely tied with the United States.

The decision to intervene militarily in 1950 reflected Truman's belief that communism must be contained globally. But such an ambitious strategy was prohibitively expensive and risky. To widen the war beyond Korea would not only be enormously costly, but might also bring about the third world war that Truman was trying to avoid in the first place. The dilemma was highlighted by General Bradley's celebrated description that the conflict in Korea must not become 'the wrong war, at the wrong place, at the wrong time and with the wrong enemy' (Bartlett, 1984, p. 302). Convinced that the invasion was part of a Soviet conspiracy, American officials feared a similar attack in Europe. Indeed, sending troops to fight in Korea was designed to impress not only America's communist foes, but also her European friends. So much diplomatic effort was expended to persuade the European allies to build up their conventional forces and to accept German rearmament, that the struggle in Korea became a virtual şideshow.

Nevertheless, the politics of the Cold War were securely fastened upon the Far East. Despite the lack of tangible evidence, the Chinese entry into the war was seen as confirmation that 'Red' China was under the control of the Soviet Union. 'The Mao Tse-tung regime is a creature of the Moscow Politburo,' declared John Foster Dulles (Graebner, 1984, p. 180). Although 13 countries, including Britain, had established diplomatic relations with the new government before June 1950, the United States refused to grant recognition. A policy of isolating Red China was adopted. Commercial and cultural relations were prohibited. At the United Nations, the American delegation resolutely opposed Red China's membership and secured the passage of a resolution condemning that government's aggression in Korea. The United States continued to recognize the nationalists in Taiwan as the legitimate government of China. Consequently, Taiwan (Republic of China) retained her seat on the Security Council, although she represented only 13 million out of a total Chinese population in excess of 500 million.

In January 1950 the Truman administration had implied that Taiwan lay outside America's defensive perimeter. Less than six months later the president affirmed that 'the occupation of Formosa by Communist forces would be a direct threat to the security of the Pacific area' (Schlesinger, 1983, IV, p. 366). The powerful American Seventh Fleet was sent to patrol the Taiwan Strait to forestall a possible invasion from the mainland. Considerable military and financial assistance was given to Chiang so that he was able to maintain himself in power and also to transform Taiwan into a formidable military stronghold. In December 1954 communist threats to seize the small islands of Quemoy and Matsu situated in the Taiwan Strait so alarmed the Eisenhower administration that it speedily entered into a defence treaty by which the United States gave a formal pledge to protect Taiwan.

The war in Korea also radically altered American relations with the other nations of the Far East. In Japan, the United States expedited the conclusion of a peace treaty in 1951 to end the occupation and restore Japanese independence. The new government of Japan immediately entered into a bilateral security agreement with the United States by which American forces were to remain in Japan for an indefinite period to provide for the nation's defence. Prior to the Korean war, George Kennan had advocated American military withdrawal from Japan, but he later concluded that 'the American military presence in Japan was wholly essential to any future security of the area' (Kennan, 1968, p. 396). For half a century the United States had sought to build up China to curb Japanese expansionism. After 1950 American policy sought an alliance with Japan to contain the spread of Chinese communism.

Meanwhile the United States had sought to build up a powerful anti-communist coalition. Defence treaties were signed with Australia, New Zealand, and the Philippines in 1951. The Eisenhower administration made the structure more formal in September 1954 by creating the Manila Pact or Southeast Asia Treaty Organization (SEATO). Intended as a Far Eastern counterpart to NATO, the new regional defence organization comprised the United States, Britain, France, Australia, New Zealand, Pakistan, Thailand, and the Philippines. In contast to NATO, however, there was no automatic commitment to use force to resist aggression. Such a stipulation would have placed an enormous burden upon the United States since she alone possessed substantial military forces. The members simply agreed to confer in the event 'of any fact or situation which might endanger the peace of the area' (Schlesinger, 1983, IV, p. 474). The limits of the alliance were further underlined by the conspicuous refusal to join of countries such as India and Indonesia.

Almost 34,000 Americans had died in the Korean war, while the number of Koreans and Chinese killed, injured, and missing numbered more than three million (Lowe, 1986, p. 218). Since the country still remained divided, the fighting appeared to have achieved little except wreak further destruction upon an already unfortunate people. Although the United States claimed that she was fighting a monolithic communist conspiracy directed from Moscow, the Soviet Union carefully avoided direct involvement. Whether Red China acted independently or was manipulated by the Soviets into joining the war, the consequences for Sino-American relations were disastrous. During the next two decades, the United States and Red China were implacable enemies. The alliance system devised by the United States to isolate Red China appeared to signify a reversal of America's traditional policy of avoiding military commitments in the Far East. America had stood up to the perceived communist challenge in Korea, but the experience of fighting a 'limited' war was financially and politically debilitating. A similar saga was repeated in Vietnam, where the consequences proved to be just as frustrating and ultimately disastrous for the United States.

The Vietnamese Domino

By the close of the nineteenth century, the region of Southeast Asia had become a French sphere of influence. The centre of France's Asian empire was Indo-China, comprising the kingdoms of Cambodia and Laos, and the three Vietnamese provinces of Annam, Tonkin, and Cochin-China. The colony was considered highly attractive because it was naturally rich in rice and rubber. It also provided an opportunity to promote France's 'civilizing mission' of instilling her traditions and culture overseas. French domination endured until 1940, when it was dramatically overthrown by Japan's military onslaught which temporarily swept away white colonial rule throughout most of East Asia.

Already demoralized by France's defeat in Europe, the French authorities in Indo-China obediently surrendered to the Japanese invaders. However, by choosing collaboration rather than resistance, French authority and prestige were fatally compromised in Indo-China. Local opposition was confined to the area close to the Chinese border in Tonkin, where guerrilla warfare was organized by a communist movement known as the Vietminh. Guided by the charismatic Ho Chi Minh and the military genius of Vo Nguyen Giap, the Vietminh emerged as a formidable political and military force in Tonkin.

After the liberation of France in 1944, rumours circulated that French troops would be sent from Europe to reconquer Indo-China. Japan reacted in March 1945 by forcibly dismissing the local French administration. Annam, Tonkin, and Cochin-China were declared united in the new state of Vietnam, which was given nominal independence under the rule of Bao Dai, the emperor of Annam. But Japan's plans were shattered by her own military surrender to the United States in August. Ho moved rapidly to fill the local vacuum of power. Claiming to represent nationalist aspirations for independence from foreign rule, Vietminh forces entered Hanoi and established a government in the name of the new Democratic Republic of Vietnam.

The bold act of declaring a republic gained support only within northern Vietnam and attracted virtually no international notice. Realizing that the United States was the most influential foreign power in the region, Ho appealed for her support. He told an American secret agent that he would welcome 'a million American soldiers ... but no French'. In a similar vein, Giap described the United States as a 'good friend' because 'it is a democracy without territorial ambitions' (Karnow, 1984, p. 147). This friendly image of the United States derived from President Roosevelt's well-known opposition to the restoration of French sovereignty in Indo-China. On one memorable occasion, he had denounced France for having 'done nothing for the Indochinese people under their care' (Thorne, 1978, p. 463).

However, the exigencies of ending the war against Japan moderated Roosevelt's anti-colonial attitude. Shortly before his death, Roosevelt even sanctioned the use of American planes to airlift small detachments of French troops within Indo-China. Moreover, Charles de Gaulle ominously warned the American ambassador at Paris in March 1945:

If the public here comes to realize that you are against us in Indochina there will be terrific disappointment and nobody knows to what that will lead. We do not want to become Communist; we do not want to fall into the Russian orbit, but I hope that you will not push us into it. (Thorne, 1978, p. 622)

Lacking Roosevelt's personal interest in Asian affairs, Truman was even less inclined to make Indo-China a divisive issue. The new president was only too pleased to receive assurances from de Gaulle that France intended to grant independence to her colonies, though this 'would inevitably be varied and gradual' (Herring, 1979, p. 111). Wishing to support France's claim to great power status, the Truman administration ignored Ho's appeals for assistance and chose instead to acquiesce in the restoration of French rule in Indo-China.

At first the French authorities were willing to consider granting a measure of local self-government to the Vietminh. Ho even visited Paris for discussions during the summer of 1946. However, friction between the Vietminh and French troops in Haiphong erupted into violence in November 1946 and sparked off the first Indo-China war, which lasted until 1954. Neither side showed any disposition to compromise. The Vietminh dedicated themselves to achieving the independence of a unified Vietnam. Outwardly, France appeared to be winning the war. The colonial administration remained intact and control was retained over the populated areas. But the influence of the Vietminh grew steadily in the north, especially among the peasants. Moreover, the constant drain of lives and money made the war increasingly unpopular in France. In 1954 the French commander, General Henri Navarre, sought a decisive test of strength at Dien Bien Phu, a remote garrison in the northwest. But he was outmanoeuvred and outnumbered by Giap. Navarre's surrender in May 1954 brought down the French government and marked the end of France's forlorn attempt to hold on to her empire in Indo-China.

Although consenting to the restoration of French rule in 1945, the Truman administration had displayed little interest in the region. American officials remained suspicious of the Vietminh, who they considered to be not nationalists but Soviet puppets. On the other hand, there was scant sympathy for French colonialism, so that requests for military assistance against the Vietminh were refused. This negative attitude was dramatically altered by the 'loss' of China and the outbreak of the Korean War. In American eyes, Indo-China was no longer the scene of a local conflict, but an integral part of the global battle to contain Soviet expansion. The Cold War perspective was further reinforced by the decision of Red China and the Soviet Union to recognize the Vietminh in 1950.

Consequently, from 1950 onwards the United States began a programme of financial assistance to France, which was steadily increased until it amounted to almost 80 per cent of French expenditure on the war.

American officials were anxious over the possible 'loss' to communism of any further countries in Asia. This fear gained the name of the 'domino theory' after President Eisenhower's remarks at a press conference in April 1954. He stated: 'You have a row of dominoes set up, you knock over the first one, and what will happen to the last one is the certainty that it will go over very quickly. So you could have a beginning of a disintegration that would have the most profound influences' (Ambrose, 1984, p. 180). Speaking as Dien Bien Phu was under siege, Eisenhower had Indo-China very much in mind. Implicit in his remarks was that the fall of Indo-China would be followed by Burma, Thailand, Malaya, and Indonesia. After Southeast Asia, communist pressure would extend to Japan, Taiwan, and the Philippines. The next dominoes would be Australia, New Zealand, and ultimately the United States herself.

Despite this frightening scenario, caution still prevailed in Washington. Both Truman and Eisenhower drew a sharp distinction between financial aid and direct American military involvement in Indo-China. Confronted with desperate pleas from Paris for an American air strike at Dien Bien Phu, Eisenhower sought not only the opinion of his military experts and leading congressmen, but also the co-operation of the British government. Several American officials, including Dulles, favoured an air strike. After careful consideration, Eisenhower ruled against military intervention. 'We cannot engage in active war,' he told Dulles (Ambrose, 1984, p. 179).

The decision provoked French bitterness, but was not quite as momentous as it appeared because the French government had already indicated its desire to negotiate a withdrawal from Indo-China. In February 1954 it had agreed to join a conference of foreign ministers at Geneva in July to discuss peace in Indo-China. Dulles was initially reluctant to attend, primarily because he regarded with distaste the presence of a delegation from Red China. Ironically, the Chinese foreign minister, Chou En-lai (Zhou Enlai), exercised a moderating influence throughout the proceedings. After the sacrifices of the Korean War, China yearned for peace and was also wary of creating an over-powerful Vietnam on her border. Moreover, the Soviet Union was concerned not to antagonize French opinion in the debate over the EDC and adopted a conciliatory attitude. Consequently, the demands of the Vietminh representative for an independent and unified Vietnam were regarded as too extreme and he was prevailed upon to accept a number of 'accords' with the French government. These stipulated an end of hostilities and the temporary division of Vietnam at the 17th parallel, pending national elections to be held within two years. It was envisaged that French troops would be withdrawn by July 1956.

While not displeased by the end of French colonial rule in Indo-China, the Eisenhower administration was unhappy at the 'loss' of northern Vietnam to communism. The American delegation at Geneva implied its assent to the accords, although it refused to grant them a formal endorsement. A statement was issued that the United States 'would view any renewal of the aggression violation of the aforesaid agreements with grave concern and as seriously threatening international peace and security' (*New York Times*, 1971, p. 52). In effect, this assertion of a protective interest in the future of Vietnam reflected the unilateral decision of the Eisenhower administration to replace the French in Indo-China. The detached policy of the past was abandoned as Eisenhower and Dulles imposed the politics of the Cold War upon Vietnam. Their declared aim was to defeat the domino theory by creating a strong and stable government in the south which would serve as a beacon of freedom in the region.

In the process, the United States steadily undermined the Geneva settlement by treating South Vietnam as a separate, sovereign state. 'While we should certainly take no positive step to speed up [the] present process of decay of Geneva accords', remarked Dulles in December 1955, 'neither should we make the slightest effort to infuse life into them' (*New York Times*, 1971, p. 23). The stipulation that Vietnam could not enter into a foreign alliance was circumvented by the inclusion of a separate protocol in the SEATO treaty of September 1954 extending protection to Vietnam. An American military mission took over from the French in 1956 and proceeded to train and equip what was intended to be a powerful South Vietnamese army.

American policy also sought to promote political stability by approving Ngo Dinh Diem's establishment of an independent Republic of Vietnam in October 1955. Fearful that national elections would result in a communist victory, no American objection was made to Diem's declaration that South Vietnam had not signed the Geneva accords and was not therefore obliged to hold elections. Instead, Diem preferred to stage his own 'national referendum' in which he won 98.2 per cent of the vote including 605,000 votes from the 405,000 voters registered in Saigon (Herring, 1979, p. 55). On his state visit to Washington in May 1957, Diem was met at the airport by Eisenhower and warmly welcomed as a redoubtable ally in the struggle against world communism.

The praise bestowed upon Diem by Eisenhower for inspiring national unity and making 'notable progress towards the great goal of constitutional government' illustrated how misinformed Americans were about Vietnam (Schlesinger, 1983, IV, p. 478). Diem's patriotism and anti-communism were not in doubt, but he was also personally a tyrant whose nepotism and devout Catholicism exacerbated Vietnamese political, religious, and cultural divisions. In 1957 a renewal of guerrilla activity was reported in the countryside. Two years later North Vietnamese military supplies and advisers were infiltrating the South via the Ho Chi Minh Trail. In essence, this marked the beginning of the second Indo-China war. Successfully exploiting Diem's unpopularity, the guerrillas steadily expanded their influence in the rural villages. In 1960 they called themselves the National Liberation Front (NLF) and declared that their aim was to overthrow Diem and reunify Vietnam. In the South, the NLF was given the name 'Vietcong'.

Although the Eisenhower administration was alarmed by the growing level of violence in South Vietnam, it was much more concerned with the Berlin crisis in Europe. Indeed, as Eisenhower left office in January 1961, he made only a passing reference about Vietnam to his successor. Nevertheless, Kennedy soon became closely involved in Vietnamese affairs. It was clear from his inaugural address that he intended to be an activist president in foreign affairs. Moreover, Vietnam suddenly acquired significance early in his administration as a result of a series of international crises in Cuba, Laos, and Berlin. Coming away from the Vienna summit meeting with Khrushchev, Kennedy believed that America's credibility as leader of the free world was in question. 'Now we have a problem in making our power credible, and Vietnam is the place,' he told an American reporter (Karnow, 1984, p. 248).

Assisted by an administration that contained some of the 'best and brightest' minds of their generation, Kennedy approached the task more as a challenge than a burden. Indeed, Vietnam presented an opportunity to implement the fashionable strategy of 'flexible response', in which communist guerrillas would be destroyed by counter-insurgency operations. Teams of 'advisers' were sent to teach the new tactics to the South Vietnamese army. Emphasis was placed not on combat, but winning the minds of the peasants. Despite official optimism, the initial results were disappointing. More and more American assistance was required, even extending to the provision of tactical air support for the South Vietnamese army. The number of American advisers markedly increased from 685 in 1981 to almost 16,000 in 1963 (*New York Times*, 1971, p. 83).

The dilemma facing American policy was summed up in two televised interviews given by President Kennedy in September 1963. In words reminiscent of Acheson's *China White Paper*, Kennedy emphasized the critical role of the people of Vietnam:

In the final analysis, it is their war. They are the ones who have to win it or lose it. We can help them, we can give them equipment, we can send our men out there as advisers, but they have to win it – the people of Vietnam – against the Communists. (Schlesinger, 1983, IV, p. 483)

A week later, when asked whether he believed in the domino theory, the president replied:

I believe it. I think that the struggle is close enough. China is so large, looms so high just beyond the frontiers, that if South Vietnam went, it would not only give them an improved geographic position for a guerrilla assault on Malaya but would also give the impression that the wave of the future in Southeast Asia was China and the Communists. So I believe it. (Schlesinger, 1983, IV, p. 484)

Whatever his own personal misgivings, Kennedy felt obliged to subscribe to the rhetoric of the Cold War. He judged that withdrawal from South Vietnam would destroy America's credibility overseas and rekindle McCarthyism at home. His decision to increase American military involvement only ensured, however, that the United States sank further into the quagmire of Vietnam.

Kennedy secretly feared that American intervention might grow to such a point that an internal Asian conflict would be transformed into an American war (Schlesinger, 1965, p. 848). This stage was reached not during his own presidency, but during that of his successor, Lyndon Johnson. On assuming office after Kennedy's assassination in 1963, Johnson reacted to gloomy news from South Vietnam with the declaration that he had no intention of being 'the first American President to lose a war' (Graebner, 1984, p. 234). His strategy was to escalate the war militarily until the enemy was forced to admit defeat. In 1964 Johnson ordered the first of many massive bombing raids on North Vietnam. Adopting the tactics of 'search and destroy', American troops assumed a direct combat role against the Vietcong. By 1968 more than 500,000 American servicemen were stationed in South Vietnam.

Johnson hoped to win the war quickly at minimum financial cost. In 1965 his advisers estimated that America's military effort would require an annual expenditure of $2 billion. Within two years the United States was spending this same amount per month! (Karnow, 1984, p. 387). Moreover, despite optimistic official reports, the expected military victory was not forthcoming. 'The Vietnamese people will never give way to force,' defiantly asserted Ho Chi Minh (Schlesinger, 1983, IV, p. 519). The predominantly agrarian economy of North Vietnam presented few significant targets for American air strikes. Instead of lowering the enemy's morale, the policy of escalation merely stimulated North Vietnamese determination to continue the war and to increase infiltration into the South. Saturation bombing by B-52s looked impressive, but was surprisingly ineffective in closing the supply routes along the Ho Chi Minh Trail. Even American officials admitted that the number of North Vietnamese troops entering the South actually tripled from 1965 to 1967 (Karnow, 1984, p. 455).

As Johnson escalated the war, the American presence in South Vietnam became so overwhelming that the authority of the government in Saigon was critically undermined. Moreover, the assassination of Diem in 1963 had resulted in a succession of political crises and military coups. Americans began to question why their country was fighting to preserve a repressive government which did not appear to have the support of its own people. Furthermore, American consciousness of the war was heightened not only by the mounting cost in casualties and money, but also by television newsreels which conveyed daily pictures of brutality and horror. Incidents such as the dropping of napalm by American planes and the slaughter of women and children at Mylai by American marines provoked a sense of moral confusion and outrage. By 1968 criticism of America's involvement in the war resounded throughout Congress and the media. Large anti-war demonstrations were organized in American cities and on college campuses.

Since the enunciation of the Truman Doctrine in 1947, American foreign policy had enjoyed the support of American public opinion. This Cold War 'consensus' collapsed, however, amid the trauma of Vietnam. The domino theory was no longer regarded as axiomatic. If Vietnam was so crucial to the defence of the United States, critics asked, why had the president not sought a declaration of war? It was also difficult to believe that the real enemies were the Soviet Union and China. Both these powers were known to be engaged in their own bitter ideological dispute. Although they gave considerable assistance to North Vietnam, this stopped short of direct military participation. Indeed, it was to the advantage of the communist powers to refrain from provocative actions and simply watch the United States sink into the Vietnamese quagmire.

With the exception of Korea, American presidents had consistently sought to avoid committing American troops to a war on the Asian mainland. Johnson's reversal of this tradition proved a disastrous miscalculation. The president viewed the struggle in Vietnam as a 'limited' war in which American power would soon prevail. The enemy, however, was much more formidable than had been anticipated. Despite suffering enormous losses and damage, North Vietnam remained totally committed to the struggle for national liberation and the unification of Vietnam. 'We will not grow tired,' Johnson had declared in April 1965 (Schlesinger, 1983, IV, p. 496). But it was the United States that found the cost of escalation unacceptable. The turning point came in January 1968 when the Vietcong launched the Tet Offensive. The surprise attack was defeated, but not before it had dealt an enormous psychological blow to American confidence about winning the war. A forlorn President Johnson felt compelled to reverse the policy of escalation and to retire from politics in 1969. It was left to his successor, Richard Nixon, to end the second Indo-China war in 1973 by negotiating American withdrawal disguised as 'peace with honour'. In reality, a humiliated United States had abandoned South Vietnam. Two years later North Vietnamese troops seized Saigon and forcibly united the two Vietnams. To perpetuate the memory of Ho, who had died in 1969, Saigon was renamed Ho Chi Minh City. It was a fitting tribute to the man who had for so long led and inspired the arduous struggle for national liberation.

4 Revolution in the Third World

The United Nations

It was natural that the leaders of the Big Three should wish to continue their wartime co-operation into the postwar world. Churchill and Stalin thought in terms of a traditional concert of great powers who would rule and divide the world among themselves. Roosevelt's views were initially similar, but he eventually gave his support to the formation of an international organization to ensure the maintenance of peace. In conferences at Dumbarton Oaks and San Francisco, the Americans took the initiative and proposed what amounted to an expanded version of the old League of Nations. 'We must provide the machinery', stated President Truman in April 1945, 'which will make future peace, not only possible, but certain' (Schlesinger, 1983, V, p. 28). The new body was called the United Nations Organization (UN) and membership was open to all independent countries. The very name 'United Nations' conveyed the sense of a common endeavour in world democracy and co-operation.

This idealist concept was soon undermined by the realities of power politics. While Americans were enthusiastic, the Soviets were suspicious of an organization created and likely to be dominated by the West. In order to ensure Soviet membership, various concessions were necessary. The most significant was the superior executive role accorded to the Security Council and the granting of the power of veto to its five permanent members. This placed Britain, China, France, the Soviet Union, and the United States in a privileged position compared to the ordinary members who formed the General Assembly. By using their veto, any one of the great powers could prevent the United Nations taking a decision which that power considered detrimental to its national interest.

Soviet misgivings were justifed because the organization was indeed dominated by the Western powers, especially the United States. Symbolic of this was the location of the United Nations' headquarters in New York. Of the initial 51 members, only five were communist countries. The large number of Latin American nations generally supported the United States. Similarly, most of the Commonwealth countries invariably voted with Britain. The West could therefore expect a large majority in both the Security Council and the General Assembly. Moreover, American influence was further heightened by the fact that the United States provided a substantial amount of the funds for agencies such as the United Nations Relief and Rehabilitation Agency (UNRRA) and possessed a virtual controlling interest in adjunct economic institutions such as the International Monetary Fund (IMF) and the World Bank.

The conflict of interests between West and East surfaced at the very first meetings of the United Nations in 1946, when controversy erupted over the admission of Argentina and Poland. Despite Soviet criticism of Argentina's fascist government, Argentine membership was accepted, while the Polish application was deferred. The Soviets were further disconcerted by Iran's request that the Security Council investigate the Soviet occupation of Azerbaijan. What had been intended as a forum for discussion and negotiation became an arena for confrontation between the great powers. Since the West would invariably win any vote, the Soviet Union resorted to the frequent use of the veto. Between 1946 and 1969 the Soviets issued 105 vetoes. Soviet displeasure even extended to a boycott of the Security Council for six months in 1950.

On occasion, the superpowers agreed that the United Nations could serve a useful peace-keeping function, as in Palestine or Kashmir. However, far from prompting a spirit of compromise, the raising of Cold War issues at the United Nations provoked only bitter and sterile debates. A notable change came about during the late 1950s when the agenda of subjects under discussion was significantly broadened. As a result of the dissolution of the European colonial empires, a large number of newly independent nations was created. By 1960 the original membership of the United Nations had almost doubled. Moreover, a majority of the members now belonged to Africa and Asia. The balance of voting power was rapidly shifting against the West. This was demonstrated by the desire of the new nations in the General Assembly to pass resolutions condemning French policy in North Africa and the alleged violation of human rights in South Africa.

As a nation who had won her own independence from colonial rule, the United States was a longstanding champion of self-determination. During the war, Roosevelt had frequently clashed with Churchill over colonial questions. In the president's opinion, more than a billion 'brown people' resented being ruled by a handful of whites. 'Our goal must be to help them achieve independence,' he said in March 1945 (Thorne, 1978, p. 594). The Truman administration upheld the rights of small nations in the United Nations and put diplomatic pressure on Britain and Holland to grant independence to India and Indonesia. But the United States was also the ally and associate of the European powers. Her financial support for France in Indo-China demonstrated that strategic interests outweighed anti-colonial sentiment. Moreover, American diplomats represented the world's leading capitalist nation and appeared uncomfortable when confronted with revolutionary political change. Citing the example of Indonesia, Acheson noted that independence was not an end, but 'a beginning of new troubles as tragic and bloody as any experienced in the past' (Acheson, 1970, p. 331). It was not surprising that many of the new countries should be suspicious of the United States and would liken American 'imperialism' to European colonialism.

While the Soviet Union firmly resisted political reform in Eastern Europe, she sought to promote radical change in the wider world by exploiting anti-Western nationalism in Africa and Asia. Amid a fanfare of publicity, Khrushchev and Bulganin initiated the new policy by visiting India, Burma, and Afghanistan in 1955. A programme of foreign aid was unveiled and close relations were subsequently cultivated with influential countries such as India and Egypt. Soviet officials pledged their support for wars of national liberation against the Western 'imperialists' and 'warmongers'. These ideas were forcefully expressed in a speech delivered by Khrushchev in 1961:

The national-liberation movement is an anti-imperialist movement. With the collapse of the colonial system, imperialism has become considerably weaker. Vast territories and enormous masses of people have ceased or are ceasing to serve as a reserve for it, as a source of cheap raw materials and cannon fodder. With the support of the socialist states and all international progressive forces, the Asian, African and Latin American countries are more and more frequently inflicting defeats on the imperialist powers and coalitions. (Schlesinger, 1983, II, p. 659)

The United States responded by increasing her foreign assistance to neutral countries such as India, Indonesia, and Yugoslavia. But the American Congress invariably sought to tie aid with political and military strings. The Soviets deliberately adopted a more even-handed posture. Not tainted by links with the former colonial masters, Soviet policy appeared more disinterested and sympathetic.

For ideological and practical reasons, communism possessed many attractions for the new states. The example of the Chinese revolution was particularly pertinent. But the most relevant and appealing model of international behaviour was provided by India. After gaining independence from Britain in 1947, India remained attached to the British Commonwealth, but insisted on pursuing an independent foreign policy. By refusing to choose between East and West, India assumed the role of leader of the 'Third World'. This approach to world politics was also described as 'neutralism' or 'non-alignment'. Its popularity was demonstrated in 1955 when 29 neutral countries attended the Bandung conference. A second meeting was held at Belgrade in 1961. A new bloc of nations emerged which found the problems of economic development more compelling than the politics of the Cold War. They feared external interference in their affairs and sought to avoid this by not becoming embroiled in the conflicts between the superpowers.

Despite a basic lack of financial and military power, the nations of the Third World found strength in their common sense of identity and their increasing numbers. They soon discovered that their majority in the General Assembly of the United Nations could have an impact on international affairs. In the process, they revitalized the economic and cultural agencies of the United Nations. On political issues, the battle against colonialism naturally absorbed the attention of the new members. But their strident attacks upon the

69

ex-colonial masters brought the Third World into a tactical alliance with the communist nations and thereby fixed an anti-Western bias upon neutralism. For example, the admission of 16 new African states in 1960 and Khrushchev's presence at the opening session of the 15th General Assembly occasioned the formulation of Resolution 1514, which affirmed that 'an end must be put to colonialism and all practices of segregation and discrimination associated therewith' (Schlesinger, 1983, V, p. 476). There were 90 votes cast in favour of the resolution, with none against. The eight nations which abstained included the United States, Britain, France, Portugal and South Africa.

The vote on Resolution 1514 demonstrated that the era of Western domination of the United Nations was over. From the point of view of the United States, the United Nations had become an instrument of demagoguery and anti-Western propaganda. The wheel had turned full circle. During the late 1940s, the Soviet Union had sought to detach herself from the United Nations. But with the notable exception of the crisis in the Congo, it was the United States who pursued a strategy of disengagement from the 1960s onwards. The founders of the United Nations had envisaged an instrument to preserve world peace. But the conflict of interests between the great powers ensured that the United Nations was effectively deprived of power. It became therefore an institution to distribute economic and cultural welfare and a platform for political propaganda. When it came to substantive discussions on Cold War issues, the superpowers preferred to deal directly between themselves.

The Middle East

Stretching from the Indian Ocean to the Mediterranean along the Red Sea, the Middle East has long provided the gateway between Asia and Europe. During the nineteenth century, its strategic and economic value made it an area of contentious international rivalry between Britain, France, and Russia. This importance was enhanced by the opening of the Suez Canal in 1869 and the discovery and development in the twentieth century of vast oilfields. Foreign penetration was aided by Arab disunity and the political instability resulting from the slow decline of the Ottoman empire. An additional source of tension was the emergence of bitter hostility between Arabs and Jews arising from the creation of the state of Israel in 1948.

At the close of the Second World War, Britain was regarded as the dominant foreign power in the Middle East. It was soon apparent, however, that British economic and military resources were seriously overextended. By 1948 Britain had evacuated Palestine and was under pressure from Egypt to withdraw from the canal zone. Historically, the United States had shown little interest in the Middle East, but American officials were alarmed that British weakness would encourage Soviet expansion. Consequently, Stalin's diplomatic demands on Turkey to negotiate a defence treaty and the maintenance of Soviet troops in northern Iran were viewed with grave suspicion in Washington. 'In picking the Straits and Iran as points of pressure', noted Dean Acheson, 'they [the Soviets] followed the route of invasion by barbarians against classical Greece and Rome and later of the czars to warm water' (1970, p. 197). To counter the perceived Soviet threat, the Truman administration broke with American diplomatic tradition and became actively involved in the affairs of the Middle East. The politics of the Cold War were therefore thrust upon the region. 'Should we fail to aid Greece and Turkey in this fateful hour,' warned Truman in March 1947, 'the effect will be far reaching to the West as well as to the East' (Schlesinger, 1983, I, p. 114).

Preoccupied with domestic reconstruction, Stalin preferred to avoid a confrontation with the United States over the Middle East. Although the sense of urgency was removed, American officials continued to remain vigilant. In terms of strategic priority, the region was ranked ahead of the Far East and second only to Europe. This would later be underlined by the stationing of the powerful Sixth Fleet in the Mediterranean. Special attention was paid to developing friendly diplomatic relations with oil-rich Saudi Arabia and Iran. Much more controversial, however, was the decision of the Truman administration to recognize the state of Israel only ten minutes after that country's declaration of independence on 14 May 1948. 'There's no Arab vote in America but there's a very heavy Jewish vote and the Americans are always having elections,' explained the British prime minister, Clement Attlee (LaFeber, 1976, p. 79).

71

American officials also realized the need for close diplomatic co-operation with Britain and France. Fearing the outbreak of an arms race between the Arabs and Israelis, the three powers joined together in 1950 to issue the Tripartite Declaration which attempted to restrict sales of military equipment. John Foster Dulles also unveiled an ambitious plan to include the region in his world-wide system of alliances designed to contain Soviet communism. He envisaged a Middle Eastern Defence Organization (MEDO) which would run along the Soviet border from the Mediterranean to the Himalayas. But the concept foundered on Egyptian resistance. Although MEDO never actually came into being, a smaller regional grouping was eventually formed by Britain in 1955. It was initially known as the Baghdad Pact and later renamed the Central Treaty Organization (CENTO). The only Arab member was Iraq.

The role of Egypt was crucial. Under the leadership of Gamal Abdel Nasser, the country presented a model of revolutionary nationalism. One of Nasser's immediate aims was the restoration of full Egyptian sovereignty over the Suez Canal zone. As he battled against foreign 'imperialism', Nasser became a spokesman for Pan-Arab unity and a leading figure in the Third World. Fearing the spread of further unrest in their colonies, Britain and France adopted a hostile attitude towards Nasser. Moreover, their dependence on supplies of oil from the Middle East made the Suez Canal a matter of vital national importance. The United States, however, was able to take a more sympathetic view in keeping with her anti-colonialist tradition. The Eisenhower administration also wished to prevent Nasser from turning to the Soviet Union for support. American officials therefore looked with favour on Egypt's attempts to introduce economic reform and undertook to give financial assistance to the massive Aswan Dam irrigation project.

Dealing with Third World leaders, however, proved far from easy. A particular dilemma for the United States arose over Nasser's request for arms. The desire to befriend the Egyptian leader had to be weighed against the certainty that the weapons would be used against Israel. By insisting upon cash payment, the State Department believed that it had tactfully frustrated Nasser's plans. To the consternation of American officials, Nasser negotiated a trade deal with the Soviet Union in which the latter accepted Egyptian cotton as payment for weapons delivered from Czechoslovakia. When Egypt recognized Red China in May 1956, Dulles was irate. In July the Americans demonstrated their displeasure by withdrawing their pledge of financial support for the Aswan Dam.

A week later Nasser again totally confounded American calculations by announcing the nationalization of the company which controlled and operated the Suez Canal. The governments of Britain and France protested on behalf of their citizens, who were the principal shareholders. After three months of desultory negotiations, hostilities erupted in late October 1956. British and French forces seized the canal, while Israel launched an offensive from the east. Eisenhower considered that military intervention was 'a terrible mistake' (Ambrose, 1984, p. 365). He was critical of Nasser, but believed that Egypt's action was legally correct. The United States would not endorse the use of force and proceeded to apply economic pressure on Britain and France to terminate their invasion. Beset by financial and political crisis, the governments of Britain and France reluctantly accepted an American plan for a ceasefire to be implemented by the United Nations.

Eisenhower's desire to bring a speedy end to the conflict was also motivated by his constant anxiety that the Soviet Union would 'make mischief' (Ambrose, 1984, p. 338). However statesmanlike the president's approach, its immediate results were disastrous for the West. Britain and France were humiliated, while Israel was angered at having to give up her conquest of the Gaza Strip. On the other hand, Egyptian control of the canal was reinstated and Nasser was acclaimed as a hero throughout the Arab world. Moreover, Khrushchev gratefully seized the opportunity to divert attention from Soviet repression of the Hungarian rebels. He boasted to the international press that his threats to fire missiles at London had compelled the British and French to withdraw. As a sign of the new relationship between Moscow and Cairo, Khrushchev stated that the Soviets would finance the Aswan Dam.

The Suez crisis therefore divided the Western powers, enhanced the reputation of Nasser, and stimulated the rise of Soviet influence in the Arab world. In order to salvage America's prestige, Eisenhower announced on 5 January 1957 what would become known as the 'Eisenhower Doctrine'. He stated categorically that

73

America supported 'without reservation the full sovereignty and independence of each and every nation of the Middle East'. Pointing out the danger to the region posed by communism, he asked for congressional authority to use 'the armed forces of the United States' to assist those countries who requested aid 'against overt armed aggression from any nation controlled by international communism' (Schlesinger, 1983, V, pp. 408–12).

Like Monroe in 1823 and Truman in 1947, Eisenhower unilaterally declared that the United States would protect substantial parts of the globe against dangers which she alone defined. Predictably, the Soviet Union condemned Eisenhower's 'crude threat to employ force' (Schlesinger, 1983, II, p. 581). But the Cold War perspective was highly misleading. The actions of the superpowers were not responsible for the political turbulence of the Middle East. The ruling Arab elites resented foreign interference, but they were much more concerned with the threat of revolutionary change and Egyptian hegemony implicit in Nasser's Pan-Arab movement. Right-wing regimes such as Lebanon, Jordan, and Saudi Arabia welcomed the Eisenhower Doctrine, which they correctly interpreted as seeking to maintain the status quo.

Nasser retaliated by condemning American meddling. He found it easy to whip up anti-American sentiment by making scathing reference to the 'special' relationship existing between the United States and Israel. Egypt and her allies in Syria and Iraq looked to the Soviet Union for military and financial assistance. Khrushchev was only too keen to comply. Such requests suited perfectly his strategy of undermining the West by backing national liberation movements in the Third World. The United States responded by expanding its aid programmes to governments which she considered friendly. But the nations of the Middle East were not transformed into satellites of the superpowers. Increasing oil revenues gave the Arab states not only a greater sense of self-esteem, but also the financial resources to prepare for war against Israel. The superpowers might supply the weapons, but they did not provide the motivation for the Arab–Israeli struggle. With the exception of the brief American military intervention in Lebanon in 1958, both superpowers were careful not to become active participants in the succession of internal crises which affected the region.

After the Portuguese voyages of discovery in the fifteenth century, Sub-Saharan Africa experienced a succession of European invaders 'scrambling' for slaves, trade, and territorial dominion. By the middle of the twentieth century, Britain, France, and Portugal possessed the largest empires, with a Belgian outpost in the Congo. Despite its size and large population, Sub-Saharan Africa remained the 'dark' continent to the rest of the world. The European powers jealously guarded their colonies and kept them out of the mainstream of international politics.

For the superpowers, Sub-Saharan Africa was a remote and scarcely known land which was assigned a low strategic priority. The United States had shown a particular interest in developing Liberia as a homeland for ex-slaves, but had maintained relatively little political and economic contact with the rest of the continent. In accordance with their universal principles, American diplomats advocated an end to colonial rule. On the other hand, they generally subscribed to the view prevailing in the West that the vast majority of black Africans had barely emerged from the Stone Age and were not ready for self-government. 'The United States Government has always maintained', stated Assistant Secretary of State George McGhee in 1951, 'that premature independence for primitive, uneducated peoples can do them more harm than good' (Schlesinger, 1983, V, p. 552).

Moreover, the colonial powers were also America's closest allies and were extremely sensitive to external interference. Consequently, American officials preferred not to encroach on what was a traditional European sphere of influence. Indeed, in contrast to other parts of the globe, Sub-Saharan Africa exhibited remarkable political stability in the years immediately following the close of the Second World War. However distasteful in principle, American officials acknowledged that European colonial rule made the continent safe from communist infiltration. 'In these troubled times', observed McGhee, 'it is gratifying to be able to single out a region of 10 million square miles in which no significant inroads have been made by communism, and to be able to characterize the area as relatively stable and secure' (Schlesinger, 1983, V, p. 549).

The deceptive calm was shattered from the mid-1950s onwards

75

as the process of decolonization gathered momentum. Starting with Ghana in 1957, most of Africa gained independence within less than a decade. The new states identified with the Third World and sought to adopt a neutral stance in international affairs. There was considerable support for a Pan-African grouping, which ultimately found expression in the formation of the Organization for African Unity (OAU) in 1963. The 32 original members, however, were united in name only. Drawn from North, West, Central, and East Africa, the OAU presented a panorama of ethnic diversity. Political differences were exacerbated by cultural barriers. Although they professed non-alignment, economic weakness meant that most countries remained closely tied to the economies of their former colonial rulers. One means of escaping from this state of dependency was to cultivate relations with the superpowers. But the United States and the Soviet Union responded cautiously. So long as there was no major disturbance, they regarded Africa as an area of minor strategic significance.

It was the crisis in the Congo (Zaïre) that thrust Africa temporarily into the centre of Cold War politics. This huge country was granted independence by Belgium on 30 June 1960. But few preparations had been made for the transition from colonial rule to self-government. Almost immediately there were reports of violent disorder. On 5 July the army mutinied and chaos ensued. The rich southern province of Katanga attempted to secede under the leadership of Moise Tshombe. The Congolese prime minister, Patrice Lumumba, appealed to the United Nations for assistance to restore order. Prompted by the UN secretary general, Dag Hammarskjöld, the Security Council agreed to despatch a peace-keeping force. American transport planes were made available to airlift UN troops into Léopoldville (Kinshasa). On 15 July the first detachments arrived out of a force which would eventually number 20,000. The largest contingents were initially drawn from Morocco, Tunisia, and Ethiopia.

Lumumba also travelled to Washington to solicit military aid. The Eisenhower administration was suspicious of his left-wing views and considered him 'an individual whom it was impossible to deal with' (Ambrose, 1984, p. 586). Rebuffed in the United States, Lumumba turned to the Soviet Union. Khrushchev pledged support and proceeded to send 'technicians' and military equipment to the Congo. The Soviet leader justified his action by alleging that the Western powers were colluding with Hammarskjöld to destroy Congolese independence. When Lumumba accused the UN peace-keeping force of openly sympathizing with his political rivals, American officials believed that a communist coup was imminent. Their policy was to back the United Nations to the hilt. 'We believe that the only way to keep the cold war out of the Congo is to keep the United Nations in the Congo,' summed up Adlai Stevenson, the American representative at the United Nations (Schlesinger, 1983, V, p. 901).

Although the pattern of political events in the Congo was confused, the outcome appeared to vindicate American strategy. In September 1960 Lumumba fell from power, and was murdered four months later. American complicity was suspected, but never fully substantiated. Whatever the reasons for his death, the event signalled the decline of Soviet influence. Soviet technicians proved ill-suited to Africa and were soon required to leave. Largely financed and equipped by the United States, the UN peace-keeping force was instrumental in restoring public order and allowing pro-Western Congolese leaders to gain political control. President Kennedy also gave his full support to the military actions which defeated the attempted secession of Katanga. For the United States, it was a controversial and expensive operation which so provoked Khrushchev's fury that the whole future of the United Nations was called into question. Much to American relief, the Soviet leader preferred diplomatic bluster rather than a military confrontation in the heart of Africa.

Wishing to keep Cold War politics out of their continent, the majority of African nations approved Kennedy's desire that the crisis in the Congo be resolved by the United Nations. They were also pleased by the president's personal interest in their affairs. Indeed, he was already famous for his speech delivered to the Senate in 1957 in which he had criticized French repression of Algerian nationalism. One of his first acts on becoming president in 1961 was to appoint G. Mennen Williams to the newly-created post of assistant secretary of state' for African affairs. To illustrate the new importance attached to Africa, Williams frequently reminded audiences of an important part of the president's inaugural address: 'To those people in the huts and villages of half the globe struggling

77

to break the bonds of mass misery we pledge our best efforts to help them help themselves, for whatever period is required – not because the Communists may be doing it, not because we seek their votes but because it is right' (Schlesinger, 1983, V, p. 638).

Under Kennedy's prompting, American economic aid to Africa rose from $100 million in 1958 to almost $380 million in 1962. Although the increase looked impressive, the amount for 1962 represented no more than 11 per cent of total American aid to developing countries (Schlesinger, 1983, V, p. 546). The reality was that American priorities lay in Europe and especially in Southeast Asia. It was acknowledged that European governments had more experience of Africa and were more capable of mounting effective aid programmes. Moreover, the emerging American interest in Africa diminished sharply after Kennedy's death in 1963. The frequent changes of government, often by military coups, also tarnished the continent's image in the United States. Criticism emerged in Congress that American aid for such projects as the Volta Dam in Ghana was misguidedly giving support to repressive regimes. However rich Africa might potentially be in raw materials and minerals, it was relatively insignificant in terms of global trade and investment. American businessmen directed most of their interest and investment not to the needy nations of black Africa, but to the affluent white-ruled republic of South Africa.

The Soviet Union condemned the United States for maintaining close relations with South Africa. Resolutions critical of South Africa's continued presence in Namibia and her racial policy of apartheid were regularly debated in the General Assembly of the United Nations and proved embarrassing to the United States. Yet Soviet influence in Sub-Saharan Africa did not markedly increase. Indeed, humiliating reverses were suffered when Soviet missions were expelled from the Congo in 1960 and from Guinea during the following year. In addition, the Soviets faced competition from the Red Chinese who established a foothold in East Africa. American officials believed that the communists were too officious and aggressive. In 1963 Mennen Williams observed that 'the Communists have to date failed to subvert or capture any African country as a satellite' (Schlesinger, 1983, V, p. 823). After several generations of foreign rule, the new African states were determined to remain free. Non-alignment was the sensible policy to adopt in world affairs. So long as their continent lacked economic and strategic significance for the superpowers, the African nations could remain relatively detached from the Cold War.

Latin America

For almost three centuries Spain and Portugal enforced international isolation upon their colonies in the New World. At the beginning of the nineteenth century the Latin American countries won their independence, but they lacked the power to become a force in world affairs. Indeed, there were so many changes of government that the region acquired a reputation for political disorder and economic mismanagement. European reconquest was prevented, however, by the ability of the new nations to defend themselves and the proprietary interest shown by the United States in her 'sister' republics. In 1823 President James Monroe declared what amounted to a warning to European powers not to meddle in the political affairs of Latin America. The statement evolved into the Monroe Doctrine and its impact was steadily reinforced by America's remarkable political, economic, and military development. The European powers came to recognize not only that American pre-eminence in the western hemisphere was a reality, but also that it provided an invaluable force for stability in what was regarded as a remote and unruly region of the world.

A complicated relationship existed between the United States and the Latin American nations. Although they resided in the same hemisphere, the two peoples were divided by ethnic, linguistic, and religious differences. Latin Americans admired the achievements of the great northern republic. But they also resented their growing subordination to the 'Yankees'. Most of all, they deplored American military intervention in the countries of the Caribbean area, such as Cuba, Nicaragua, and Panama. However, the Latin American nations were too weak and divided among themselves to challenge the supremacy of the United States. During the economic depression of the 1930s, they welcomed American economic assistance and responded warmly to Roosevelt's declaration that his country would act as a 'good neighbour'. Pan-American solidarity was also strengthened by the threat of fascist aggression. The United States took the lead in organizing hemispheric defence and persuaded the majority of the Latin American countries to join the Second World War. The war effort itself was financed and administered from Washington. The Latin Americans mainly supplied raw materials and military bases. While the economic benefits were considerable, their dependence upon the United States noticeably increased.

The Latin American governments hoped that close cooperation with the United States would continue after the war. Indeed, American assistance was considered vital to promote economic development, which would combat the massive problems of exploding population growth and the rising expectations for a higher standard of living and social justice. During the war, however, it was evident that the United States was becoming more preoccupied with Europe and the Far East. After 1945 the United States abandoned her traditional isolationism and took on world-wide commitments. In the process, a policy of neglect was adopted towards Latin America. Latin Americans complained that there was no Marshall Plan for them. In reply, American diplomats preached the values of self-help and private enterprise. Secretary of State Marshall explained in 1948:

My Government is prepared to increase the scale of assistance it has been giving to the economic development of the American republics. But it is beyond the capacity of the United States Government itself to finance more than a small portion of the vast development needed. The capital required through the years must come from private sources, both domestic and foreign. (Schlesinger, 1983, III, pp. 45–6)

While avoiding discussion of economic matters, American officials displayed much keener interest in asserting their country's exclusive political and military leadership of the hemisphere. A system of collective security was established in 1947 by the Inter-American Treaty for Reciprocal Assistance (the Rio Pact). Article three of the treaty foreshadowed NATO by providing 'that an armed attack by any State against an American State shall be considered as an attack against all the American States' (Schlesinger, 1983, III, p. 31). During the following year, the Organization of American States (OAS) was created in accordance with article 52 of the UN Charter, which allowed member states to enter into separate regional organizations to deal with local security problems. By ensuring that inter-American disputes would be first submitted to the OAS rather than the United Nations, the United States sought to insulate Latin America from outside political influences.

The countries of Latin America also had a role to play in the emerging Cold War against the Soviet Union. On welcoming the Latin American foreign ministers to a conference at Washington in March 1951, President Truman noted that their purpose was 'to work out ways and means by which our united strength may be employed in the struggle for freedom throughout the world' (Schlesinger, 1983, III, pp. 140–1). Although the area was considered secure from external communist aggression, military assistance programmes were developed after 1951 so that the Latin American governments would assume a larger share of the burden of hemispheric defence. 'By doing this we can release thousands of U.S. soldiers for other duty,' noted the State Department in 1953 (1983, III, p. 176). While outwardly in favour of democratic governments, the United States found it easier to work with authoritarian regimes, such as Batista in Cuba and the Somoza family in Nicaragua, who shared America's anti-communist ethos.

In the era of McCarthyism, it was not surprising that American officials were disturbed by the rise of revolutionary nationalism in Latin America. The talk of land reform, greater power for trades unions, and nationalization of foreign companies was not a new phenomenon, but it was now attributed to communist subversion. This was most marked in Guatemala, where attempts to confiscate the property of the United Fruit Company were seen as instigated by local communists who had infiltrated into influential positions in the government and the trades unions. The Eisenhower administration feared that a Soviet satellite would be created in Central America and placed increasing pressue on the Guatemalan government to remove communists from office. When President Jacobo Arbenz purchased weapons from Czechoslovakia in 1954, Secretary of State Dulles ominously warned that 'international communism is making great efforts to extend its political control to this hemisphere'. Less than three months later in June 1954, a small army of political exiles equipped and organized in Honduras by the Central Intelligence Agency (CIA) staged a military coup to bring down Arbenz. Dulles claimed that the Guatemalan people had determined events and that the country's future would now be directed by 'loyal' leaders 'who have not treasonably become the agents of an alien despotism which sought to use Guatemala for its own evil ends' (Schlesinger, 1983, III, pp. 260, 285).

Although they supported Dulles in public, Latin American governments were dismayed by America's covert use of armed force. Moreover, their cooperative attitude in the Cold War did not result in the expected economic favours from the United States. Indeed, the United States was increasingly seen as a major obstacle to political and economic reform. Not only did American officials give open support to the most brutal dictatorships, but they also were accused of colluding with their huge corporations to plunder the riches of the hemisphere. Anti-American sentiment emerged at its most virulent when a howling mob in Caracas attacked Vice-President Richard Nixon's motorcade on his 'goodwill' tour of 1958.

The Eisenhower administration was taken aback by the depth of anti-American hostility. It quickly decided to remedy affairs by significantly increasing the provision of financial aid for the region. This programme would be further expanded by President Kennedy in the form of the 'Alliance for Progress'. In the meantime, however, the United States had to deal with the rise to power in Cuba of an avowed revolutionary regime under the leadership of Fidel Castro. American officials were puzzled as to whether Castro was a communist. They were certainly concerned by his determination to decrease Cuba's dependence on the United States. Relations grew increasingly bitter when Castro nationalized American banks and signed a trade agreement with the Soviet Union. Eisenhower considered Castro 'a madman' and authorized the CIA to prepare a covert operation to overthrow him (Ambrose, 1984, p. 556). The attempt took place after Eisenhower had left office and ended in disastrous failure at the Bay of Pigs in April 1961.

The United States was humiliated, while Castro's prestige was enormously enhanced. Khrushchev pledged support and declared that the Soviet Union 'will not abandon the Cuban people' (Schlesinger, 1983, III, p. 536). Castro replied by affirming his personal adherence to Marxism–Leninism and aligning Cuba with the communist nations. While the rest of Latin America generally applauded Castro's defiant stand against American bullying, they watched with dismay as Cuba became a satellite of the Soviet Union and a base for launching guerrilla operations to overthrow governments on the mainland of South America. Even more alarming was the threat of nuclear war in the hemisphere caused by Khrushchev's recklessness in placing missiles on the island. After some initial reluctance, the Latin American nations approved American proposals to expel Cuba from the OAS and to isolate the island politically and economically.

While the Soviets successfully established a bridgehead in Cuba, they made little headway in Latin America as a whole. The Soviet Union was a remote power which had a history of minimal political and economic contact with the region. Only Argentina, Mexico, and Uruguay maintained diplomatic relations with Moscow throughout the 1950s. Indeed, the strongly Catholic societies of Latin America had an innate aversion to communism. Much to the relief of the United States, the Cuban example was not therefore directly copied elsewhere in the hemisphere. But the tide of political and economic change had not been stemmed. Disappointed by the Alliance for Progress, the Latin American nations looked beyond the United States and found more in common with the nations of the Third World. Brazil, for example, deliberately sought to cultivate friendly relations with the new African states.

American diplomats continued, however, to interpret hemispheric events in Cold War terms. In the same way that he was determined not to 'lose' South Vietnam, President Lyndon Johnson would not allow another Cuba in the hemisphere. When political chaos erupted in the Dominican Republic in 1965, he despatched more than 20,000 American troops to restore order. 'The last thing I wanted – and the last thing the American people wanted – was another Cuba on our doorstep', he explained (1972, p. 198). The intervention aroused heated controversy within the United States. Johnson was accused of exaggerating the communist threat and reacting with military overkill.

In 1965 President Johnson called on the American people to assume the role of the world's policeman not only in the Dominican Republic, but also in Vietnam. However, the military success achieved in the Caribbean was not repeated in Southeast Asia. In fact, Johnson's obsession with Vietnam prevented him from acknowledging changes in the nature of the Cold War. Since 1945 the two superpowers had dominated international politics. From the mid-1960s onwards, however, the bipolar world gave way to a more diverse international order. The preference of the Third World for non-alignment and national self-assertion was paralleled by the desire of Western Europe, China, and Japan to exercise a more active role in world affairs commensurate with their own growing power and sense of importance. The Cold War was not over and would continue so long as an adversarial relationship persisted between the United States and the Soviet Union. But the tone of the verbal battle noticeably softened as both superpowers increasingly talked of seeking *détente* rather than confrontation.

References

Acheson, Dean 1970: *Present at the creation*. London: Hamish Hamilton.

Achilles, Theodore C. 1985: The Omaha milkman. In André de Staercke (ed.), *NATO's anxious birth*. London: Hurst, 30–41.

Alperovitz, Gar 1965: *Atomic diplomacy*. New York: Simon and Schuster.

Ambrose, Stephen E. 1983a: *Rise to globalism*. London: Penguin.

Ambrose, Stephen E. 1983b: *Eisenhower*. Vol. I. New York: Simon and Schuster.

Ambrose, Stephen E. 1984: *Eisenhower*. Vol. II. London: Allen & Unwin.

Anderson, Terry H. 1981: *The United States, Great Britain, and the Cold War, 1944–1947*. Columbia: University of Missouri Press.

Bartlett, Christopher J. 1984: *The global conflict*. London: Longman.

Bernstein, Barton J. (ed.) 1970: *Politics and policies of the Truman administration*. Chicago: Quadrangle.

Calvocoressi, Peter 1982: *World politics since 1945*. London: Longman.

Clay, Lucius D. 1950: *Decision in Germany*. New York: Doubleday.

Dallek, Robert 1979: *Franklin D. Roosevelt and American foreign policy, 1932–1945*. New York: Oxford University Press.

Delmas, Claude 1985: A change of heart. In André de Staercke (ed.), *NATO's anxious birth*. London: Hurst, 61–7.

Divine, Robert A. 1981: *Eisenhower and the Cold War*. New York: Oxford University Press.

Feis, Herbert 1970: *From trust to terror*. New York: Norton.

Fleming, Denna F. 1961: *The Cold War and its origins*. 2 vols. New York: Doubleday.

Frazier, Robert 1984: Did Britain start the Cold War? *Historical Journal*, 27, 715–27.

Gaddis, John L. 1972: *The United States and the origins of the Cold War, 1941–1947*. New York: Columbia University Press.

Gaddis, John L. 1982: *Strategies of containment*. Oxford: Oxford University Press.

Gaddis, John L. 1983: The emerging post-revisionist synthesis on the origins of the Cold War. *Diplomatic History*, 7, 171–204.

Graebner, Norman A. 1984: *America as a world power*. Wilmington: Scholarly Resources.

Halle, Louis J. 1967: *The Cold War as history*. London: Chatto & Windus.

Hathaway, Robert M. 1981: *Ambiguous partnership*. New York: Columbia University Press.

Herring, George C. 1979: *America's longest war*. New York: Knopf.

Horowitz, David 1965: *The free world colossus*. New York: Hill & Wang.

Johnson, Lyndon B. 1972: *The vantage point*. London: Weidenfeld & Nicolson.

Karnow, Stanley 1984: *Vietnam*. London: Penguin.

Kennan, George F. 1968: *Memoirs 1925–1950*. London: Hutchinson.

Kolko, Gabriel 1968: *The politics of war*. London: Weidenfeld & Nicolson.

Kolko, Joyce and Gabriel 1972: *The limits of power*. London: Harper & Row.

Krock, Arthur 1968: *Memoirs*. New York: Funk & Wagnalls.

Kuklick, Bruce 1972: *American policy and the division of Germany*. Ithaca, NY: Cornell University Press.

LaFeber, Walter 1976: *America, Russia and the Cold War*. New York: Wiley.

Leffler, Melvyn P. 1984: The American conception of national security and the beginnings of the Cold War, 1945–1948. *American Historical Review*, 89, 346–400.

Lowe, Peter 1986: *The origins of the Korean War*. London: Longman.

Maddox, Robert J. 1973: *The new left and the origins of the Cold War*. Princeton: Princeton University Press.

Manchester, William 1979: *American Caesar*. London: Hutchinson.

May, Ernest R. 1973: *'Lessons' of the past*. New York: Oxford University Press.

Millis, Walter (ed.) 1951: *The Forrestal diaries*. New York: Viking.

New York Times 1971: *The Pentagon papers*. London: Routledge & Kegan Paul.

Osgood, Robert E. 1962: *NATO*. Chicago: University of Chicago Press.

Ovendale, Ritchie 1982: Britain, the U.S.A. and the European Cold War. *History*, 67, 217–36.

Paterson, Thomas G. 1979: *On every front*. New York: Norton.

Ponomaryov, B. et al. (eds) 1974: *History of Soviet foreign policy, 1945–1970*. Moscow: Progress Publishers.

Salinger, Pierre 1967: *With Kennedy*. London: Jonathan Cape.

Schlesinger, Arthur M., Jr. 1965: *A thousand days*. London: André Deutsch.

Schlesinger, Arthur M., Jr. 1967: Origins of the Cold War. *Foreign Affairs*, 46, 22–52.

86

Schlesinger, Arthur M., Jr. (ed.) 1983: *The dynamics of world power*. 5 vols. New York: Chelsea House.

Sherwin, Martin 1975: *A world destroyed*. New York: Knopf.

Siracusa, Joseph M. (ed.) 1978: *The American diplomatic revolution*. Milton Keynes: Open University Press.

Spanier, John W. 1960: *American foreign policy since World War II*. New York: Praeger.

Thomas, Hugh 1986: *Armed truce*. London: Hamish Hamilton.

Thorne, Christopher 1978: *Allies of a kind*. Oxford: Oxford University Press.

Truman, Harry S. 1955: *Year of decisions 1945*. London: Hodder and Stoughton.

Truman, Harry S. 1956: *Years of trial and hope 1946–1953*. London: Hodder and Stoughton.

Ulam, Adam B. 1973: *The rivals*. London: Allen Lane.

Walton, Richard J. 1973: *Cold War and counter-revolution*. Baltimore: Penguin.

Williams, William A. 1962: *The tragedy of American diplomacy*. New York: World Publishing.

Yergin, Daniel 1978: *Shattered peace*. London: André Deutsch.

Index

71–4, 76–8, 84; and United
Nations, 6, 17, 66–70; and Vietnam
War, 18, 56–65, 83